Princeton University

Princeton, New Jersey

Written by Alison S. Fraser
Edited by Kevin Nash

Additional contributions by Omid Gohari,
Christina Koshzow, Chris Mason, Adam Burns, Joey Rahimi,
Jon Skindzier, Luke Skurman, Tim Williams,
and Kimberly Moore

ISBN # 1-59658-100-X
ISSN # 1551-0617

Special thanks to Babs Carryer, Andy Hannah, Launch-Cyte, Tim O'Brien, Bob Sehlinger, Thomas Emerson, Andrew Skurman, Barbara Skurman, Bert Mann, Dave Lehman, Daniel Fayock, Chris Babyak, The Donald H. Jones Center for Entrepreneurship, Terry Slease, Jerry McGinnis, Bill Ecenberger, Idie McGinty, Kyle Russell, Jacque Zaremba, Larry Winderbaum, Paul Kelly, Roland Allen, Jon Reider, Team Evankovich, Julie Fenstermaker, Lauren Varacalli, Abu Noaman, Jason Putorti, Mark Exler, Daniel Steinmeyer, Jared Cohon, Gabriela Oates, Tri Ad Litho, David Koegler, and Glen Meakem.

Bounce Back Team: Akila Raman, Ita Ekpoudom, Robert Accordino

College Prowler™
5001 Baum Blvd.
Suite 456
Pittsburgh, PA 15213

Phone: (412) 697-1390, 1(800) 290-2682
Fax: (412) 697-1396, 1(800) 772-4972
E-mail: info@collegeprowler.com
Website: www.collegeprowler.com

Welcome to College Prowler™

During the writing of College Prowler's guidebooks, we felt it was critical that our content was unbiased and unaffiliated with any college or university. We think it's important that our readers get honest information and a realistic impression of the student opinions on any campus — that's why if any aspect of a particular school is terrible, we (unlike a campus brochure) intend to publish it. While we do keep an eye out for the occasional extremist — the cheerleader or the cynic — we take pride in letting the students tell it like it is. We strive to create a book that's as representative as possible of each particular campus. Our books cover both the good and the bad, and whether the survey responses point to recurring trends or a variation in opinion, these sentiments are directly and proportionally expressed through our guides.

College Prowler guidebooks are in the hands of students throughout the entire process of their creation. Because you can't make student-written guides without the students, we have students at each campus who help write, randomly survey their peers, edit, layout, and perform accuracy checks on every book that we publish. From the very beginning, student writers gather the most up-to-date stats, facts, and inside information on their colleges. They fill each section with student quotes and summarize the findings in editorial reviews. In addition, each school receives a collection of letter grades (A through F) that reflect student opinion and help to represent contentment, prominence, or satisfaction for each of our 20 specific categories. Just as in grade school, the higher the mark the more content, more prominent, or more satisfied the students are with the particular category.

Once a book is written, additional students serve as editors and check for accuracy even more extensively. Our bounce-back team — a group of randomly selected students who have no involvement with the project — are asked to read over the material in order to help ensure that the book accurately expresses every aspect of the university and its students. This same process is applied to the 200-plus schools College Prowler currently covers. Each book is the result of endless student contributions, hundreds of pages of research and writing, and countless hours of hard work. All of this has led to the creation of a student information network that stretches across the nation to every school that we cover. It's no easy accomplishment, but it's the reason that our guides are such a great resource.

When reading our books and looking at our grades, keep in mind that every college is different and that the students who make up each school are not uniform — as a result, it is important to assess schools on a case-by-case basis. Because it's impossible to summarize an entire school with a single number or description, each book provides a dialogue, not a decision, that's made up of 20 different topics and hundreds of student quotes. In the end, we hope that this guide will serve as a valuable tool in your college selection process. Enjoy!

OMID GOHARI ◯ CHRISTINA KOSHZOW ◯ CHRIS MASON ◯ JOEY RAHIMI ◯ LUKE SKURMAN ◯
Founders of College Prowler™

Table of Contents

Introduction from the Author

When I found out I would be attending Princeton University in the fall of my senior year of high school, I heard more jokes about the Ivy League and Princeton's country club reputation than I ever anticipated. Once I would get past these quips in a conversation with someone whom I had just met at a leadership conference or at a casual gathering, my new acquaintance would inevitably rattle off his or her knowledge of the University with a sense of pride, whether it was to remind me that Princeton's undergraduate program had, yet again, been ranked first in the nation by another national venue, or whether it was to share the name of a friend or family member who had attended Princeton. As a high school senior at an extremely competitive school located just miles from the University's campus, I was more than aware of Princeton's reputation but would only come to understand the significance of the Princeton experience as my graduating class walked out FitzRandolph Gates onto Nassau Street, as per tradition. The words of an alumnus whom I had encountered several days earlier reverberated in my mind, "The toughest thing about Princeton is not getting in. It is getting over it," and I realized that Princeton could never just be a top ranking.

As one of the first American universities, Princeton initially carved its reputation as a place for the emerging American upper-class to send their sons to receive a gentleman's education. A lot has changed since Princeton's founding in 1746. Princeton's diverse student body enjoys an equally varied course selection ranging from the engineering of bridges to studies of musical theatre as a literary genre. The physical plan of the University has expanded to include top athletic facilities, five residential colleges for underclassmen, the Gothic spires of upperclass housing, top dining facilities, state-of-the-art computing and classroom facilities, and vast amounts of green space for the enjoyment of the campus community. While the make-up of the University has changed significantly, Princeton's commitment to undergraduate education remains. Princeton undergrads are the focus of campus life and enjoy the attention of some of the nation's top scholars, their professors, which is unusual in a top research institution.

Perhaps it is a case of "orange and black fever" that has afflicted the professors, alumni, and students, but understanding Princeton takes knowing more than just its statistics. While it is one of the most difficult universities to acquire admission, the privilege of attendance is never forgotten in this place of strong traditions as well as forward thinking. In writing this guide, I hope I have evoked Princeton as a place of many dimensions—historical, statistical, and phenomenal—that will help you gain some insight on the true student experience at the nation's top undergraduate institution.

Alison S. Fraser, Author
Princeton University

By the Numbers

General Information

Princeton University
Princeton, NJ 08544

Control:
Private

Academic Calendar:
Semester

Religious Affiliation:
None

Founded:
1746

Website:
www.princeton.edu

Main Phone:
(609) 258-3000

Admissions Phone:
(609) 258-3060

Student Information

Full-Time Undergrads:
4,676

Part-Time Undergrads:
131

Total Male Undergrads:
2,520

Total Female Undergrads:
2,317

Female to Male Ratio:
48% to 52%

Admissions

Overall Acceptance Rate:
10%

Early Acceptance Rate:
24%

Regular Acceptance Rate:
8%

Total Applicants:
15,726

Total Acceptances:
1,601

Freshman Enrollment:
1,176

Yield (percentage of admitted students who actually enroll):
75.4%

Early Decision Available?
Yes

Early Action Available?
No

Total Early Decision Applicants:
2,120

Total Early Decision Acceptances:
585

Early Decision One Deadline:
Nov 10

Early Decision One Notification:
Dec 15

Regular Decision Deadline:
January 1

Regular Decision Notification:
April 3

Must Reply-By Date:
May 1

Common Application Accepted?
No

Supplemental Forms?
Yes

Admissions Phone:
(609) 258-3060

Admissions Website:
www.princeton.edu/Siteware/Admissions.shtml

Applicants placed on waiting list:
471

Applicants accepting a place on waiting list:
298

Students enrolled from waiting list:
27

SAT I or ACT Required?
SAT required

First-Year Students Submitting SAT Scores:
99%

SAT I Range (25th – 75th Percentile):
1370 – 1560

SAT I Verbal Range (25th – 75th Percentile):
680 – 770

SAT I Math Range (25th – 75th Percentile):
690– 790

SAT II Requirements for School of Arts and Science:
Three different subject areas

SAT II Requirements for School of Engineering:
Three different subject areas, preferably including one in either physics or chemistry and, in addition, one in either Level I or Level II mathematics

Retention Rate:
98%

Top 10% of High School Class:
94%

Application Fee:
$65

Financial Information

Tuition:
$29,910

Room and Board:
$8,387

Books and Supplies:
$990

Average Need-Based Financial Aid Package (including loans, work-study, grants, and other sources):
$25,281

Students Who Applied For Financial Aid:
53%

Students Who Applied For Financial Aid and Received It:
49%

Financial Aid Forms Deadline:
February 1

Financial Aid Phone:
(609) 258-3330

Financial Aid Website:
www.princeton.edu/pr/aid02/othmenu.shtml

Academics

The Lowdown On...
Academics

Degrees Awarded:
Bachelor
Master
Doctorate

Most Popular Areas of Study:
11% Political Science and Government
11% History
10% Economics
7% Public Policy Analysis
6% English

Undergraduate Schools:
Arts and Science
Engineering

Graduation Rate
Four-years: 91%
Five-years: 96%
Six-years: 97%

➡

Fulltime Faculty:
771

Student-to-Faculty Ratio: 5.6:1

Faculty with Terminal Degree:
94.8%

Average Course Load:
Four for A.B. students, Five for B.S.E. students

IB Test Score Requirements:

A score of 6 or 7 on the International Baccalaureate (higher level) qualifies students for AP in most subjects.

AP Test Score Requirements:

AP Test Scores may be used to (1) enter upper-level courses, (2) fulfill the foreign language requirement, (3) become eligible for graduation in three or three and one-half years (advanced standing). Generally, a score of 4 or 5 is needed to receive recognition. Princeton University does not recognize the Music, Computer Science A, Statistics, Environmental Science, Human Geography, Politics, and Psychology AP Tests. See http://www.princeton.edu/pr/admissions/u/ap/table.htm for further details.

Special Degree Options

Cross-registration, Independent Study, Study Abroad, Interdisciplinary certificate program in addition to departmental concentration, Independent Concentration, Teacher Certificate Program

Best Places to Study

Empty classrooms in the Frist Campus Center, Firestone Library, Small World Coffee, Café Vivian, Architecture Library

Sample Academic Clubs

American Institute of Chemical Engineers, Engineering Council, Finance and Economic Forum, Ivy Leaguers For Freedom, Pre-Business Society, Princeton Association of Women in Science

Did You Know?

? Princeton University's sixth president, **John Witherspoon**, was one of the signers of the Declaration of Independence.

James Madison, Class of 1771 and former president of the United States, became the first president of the Alumni Association of the College of New Jersey in 1826.

Woodrow Wilson, Class of 1879 and future President of the United States, served as thirteenth president of the University in June 1902 and revolutionized the academic program through his inventive "preceptorial" system, which is still in use today.

In May 1970, Colleges around the nation adopt the "**Princeton Plan**" (fall recess) in response to the student unrest following the Cambodian incursion in Southeast Asia.

The faculty currently includes **five recipients of the Nobel Prize** in physics, two in economic studies, and one each in literature, economic sciences, and medicine.

After Princeton's founding, it was widely speculated that there was **a curse on the university's presidents**, as there were five presidents in the first twenty years of the University.

Princeton is one of the only American institutions to **mandate a senior thesis**, which has been a requirement for graduation since 1925.

Princeton's Honor System has been in place since 1893, when students, who were dissatisfied with faculty proctoring of examinations, called for a system similar to the ones at the University of Virginia and William and Mary. Even today, there are no proctors in exams, and students must sign the honor code at the end of every assignment and exam.

Students Speak Out On...
Academics

> "The professors and preceptors are remarkably concerned with the academic life of the undergraduate both in theory and practice. The university requirements for independent work mandate close student-teacher contact and in practice, professors generally make themselves easily available to meet outside of the classroom regardless of the size of the class."

"The teachers at the school are pretty good. **There are some good lecturers and some pretty boring ones.** Most of the teachers in my electrical engineering department were very helpful and usually willing to meet with students if there were questions. Some professors couldn't teach anything, but for those, you can rely on the teaching assistants and your classmates."

"Outstanding! Princeton is all about the undergrad program. The classes are great, and the **professors actually teach them.** You can really get to know your professors if you make the extra step to try to meet them and do things like going to their office hours. That is the best part!"

"Princeton hosts a **Freshmen Seminar program**, which creates a variety of seminars open only to freshman. While the topics are narrowly-tailored, depending upon the professor's personal academic interests, this program allows freshmen to participate in intensive discussion groups and helps to ease them into the increased academic expectations of sophomore year."

Q "I loved my professors. **They are world famous**, yet they would take me to dinner to discuss the means of educating inner-city youth, the meaning of Melville's short stories, or even why New York was on one of the largest fault lines. The personal attention is great, and I still turn on my TV and see my professors on there all the time."

Q "Overall, the professors are pretty good, although **they definitely vary from good to bad.** The math department is notorious for bad instructors in introductory classes. You'll find some really outstanding teachers and probably some pretty bad ones, but most are in-between and approachable and at least try to help out the students. This doesn't mean it won't get really hard sometimes. Unfortunately, at schools like Princeton, you'll often find that the best professors in terms of research and fame are not always really good at transferring their knowledge to students. So sometimes, there ends up being a fair amount of self-learning and collaboration with other students in study groups."

Q "Teachers are pretty good. **Some TAs don't speak English too well**, but office hours are very helpful."

Q "My classes, for the most part, were fascinating, mostly because of the **enthusiasm of my professors.** The professors are extremely accessible. I had the opportunity to have both great personal and academic relationships with many of them. Most of them were interested in student life in general and were also great about getting to know students individually."

Q "Academic programs here are **the best you will find anywhere.** The reason I came here is because the focus is on the undergraduate student. Every program and department ranks among the elite in its field. I came here not knowing what I would major in, but nonetheless, I was confident that whatever I chose would be in a strong department. Some of the best professors in the world reside here at Princeton, and unlike other schools, they actually teach undergraduate courses."

Q "Teachers and academics are great. We're number one this year. There are both large and small classes, depending on what you want to take. You can get a lot of attention from professors if you want it or take small classes. **It's academically rigorous with a lot of work**, especially if you're involved in other things on campus and don't have much time to study."

Q "The Princeton faculty is particularly adept at both **adapting courses to academic and technological trends** and responding to student feedback. The result is a course offering of lectures and seminars that captivate and challenge."

Q "Princeton's **name pretty much speaks for itself** here. The academic programs and professors are, by far, the best in the country. All of the departments have world-renowned experts, and you will definitely come out with an amazing education."

Q "It's **nothing short of phenomenal.** Everyone is at the top of his or her field. Granted, some don't teach as well as others, but you can kind of find that out in advance and schedule your classes around it. You can check out the student guide online to find our student reviews on the professors."

Q "Our academic programs are first-rate, and **many of our professors are highly regarded in their fields.** Also, because of Princeton's commitment to undergraduate education, the professors are accessible to students. Of course, some of them are quite dull, but that is the exception. The academics are hands-down outstanding. It's primarily an undergraduate institution, so the professors are there for us. Professors are required to have a certain number of office hours, so students can drop by at any time during those times to talk about class, papers, etc. Most professors have more than the required hours."

The College Prowler Take On...
Academics

The level of Princeton's academics make it one of the best schools in the nation for undergraduate education, if not the best. Princeton's instructors set it aside from other Ivies. Princeton's professors are not only well-credentialed, but they also place an emphasis on personal accessibility. All professors are required to teach, and no graduate students are allowed to lead lecture courses. What results is an institution focused upon the education of undergraduates, not the research of professors. Each week, Princeton professors hold office hours so that students may stop by their offices to discuss upcoming assignments or misunderstood lecture topics. The policies of each professor vary, but, generally, students do not have to make appointments to go to office hours. Some professors, such as the famed religion professor and author of the recent "Democracy Matters," Cornel West, even ask students not to send email but instead to stop by office hours to facilitate interaction out of the classroom.

While some students gripe about some of Princeton's academic requirements, including a diverse selection of distribution requirements, demanding independent work both junior and senior years, and mandatory weekly preceptorial sections, it is these features of the undergraduate education at Princeton that make Princeton students some of the best prepared for graduate work and demanding jobs. Princeton's rigorous academic demands encourage independent thought and efficiency. Even though the work is demanding, there are many resources available to undergraduates, such as an extensive network of tutors and a staff of well-trained Writing Center advisors, that ensure that few are left behind.

A+

The College Prowler™ Grade on
Academics: A+

A high Academics grade generally indicates that Professors are knowledgeable, accessible, and genuinely interested in their students' welfare. Other determining factors include class size, how well professors communicate, and whether or not classes are engaging.

Local Atmosphere

The Lowdown On...
Local Atmosphere

Region:
Mid-Atlantic

City, State:
Princeton, New Jersey

Setting:
Suburban

Distance from Philadelphia:
1 Hour

Distance from NYC:
1 Hour

City Websites:
www.princetonol.com/
www.pacpub.com/

Points of Interest:

Albert Einstein's house (c. 1840)

112 Mercer St., Princeton

Hours: Not open to the public

The Nobel-prize winning physicist and honorary degree holder from Princeton occupied this Greek revival white frame two-story house from the time that he was forced out of his position at the Academy of Sciences in Berlin by the Nazis in the early 1930s until his death in 1955. While in Princeton, Einstein studied at Princeton's Institute for Advanced Studies and helped over two hundred European scholars, artists, and scientists who asked him for help in emigrating.

Art Museum

McCormick Hall, Princeton University

Phone: (609) 258-3787

Hours: Tuesday-Saturday, 10 a.m.-5 p.m.; Sunday, 1 p.m.-5 p.m., Free.

Princeton's Art Museum offers a collection ranging from East Asian treasures to French impressionist paintings.

Bainbridge House (1766)

158 Nassau St., Princeton

Phone: (609) 921-6748

Hours: Monday-Friday, 9 a.m.-5 p.m.; Saturday 1 p.m.-4 p.m.

Currently home to the Historical Society of Princeton, the Bainbridge House is one of the few remaining 18th-century houses in Princeton Borough. It contains rooms with period furniture and frequently presents special exhibitions.

Drumthwacket

354 Stockton St., Princeton

Phone: (609) 683-0591

Hours: Wednesday, 12 p.m.-2 p.m.

Built in 1835 by Charles Olden, a Civil War governor, Drumthwacket was restored and furnished by the New Jersey Historical Society and presently serves as the official residence of the Governor of New Jersey.

Firestone Library

Corner of Nassau St. and Washington Rd., Princeton

Phone: (609) 258-3180

Hours: Monday-Saturday, 9 a.m.-5 p.m.; Sunday 2 p.m.-5 p.m.

As Princeton's central research library, Firestone Library houses more than 4 million books, including a rich collection of rare books. Three galleries are open to the public, as is a replica of the College of New Jersey library.

Grounds for Sculpture

18 Fairgrounds Rd., Hamilton

Phone: (609) 586-0616

Hours: Tuesday-Sunday, 10 a.m.-9 p.m.

The Grounds for Sculpture is a 22-acre landscaped sculpture park on the former state fairgrounds site, with indoor exhibitions in the glass-walled, 10,000 square foot museum. In addition to a collection of modern sculpture, the artists also use the natural surroundings to recreate famous Impressionist painting scenes, such as Monet's "Water Lilies." For an upscale meal off campus, make sure to try the recently remodeled Rat's, which utilizes the sculpture park's beautiful location.

Morven

55 Stockton St., Princeton

Phone: (609) 683-4495

Hours: Wednesday, 11 a.m.-2 p.m., or by appointment. Closed in August.

Built as the home of Richard Stockton III, a signer of the Declaration of Independence, and his wife Annis Boudinot Stockton, a published poet, Morven served as one of Princeton's social hubs during the 18th century. During the Revolutionary War, it has been hypothesized that British General Cornwallis used Morven as his headquarters in 1777. The building underwent major alterations in the 1850s, and in 1954, the home was donated by the owners to the State, requiring that it be used either as a Governor's mansion or a museum. Morven was used as the Governor's home until the opening of Drumthwacket, and it is currently used as a museum.

Nassau Hall (1756)

Nassau St. at the top of Witherspoon St., Princeton University

Hours: Usually open weekdays and Sunday afternoons until 5 p.m., plus all day Saturdays. Guidebooks are available at Maclean House or the University Store.

When Nassau Hall was completed in 1756, it was the largest academic building in the colonies, and it housed the entire College of New Jersey (now Princeton University) for nearly 50 years. Nassau Hall has survived bombardment during the Revolutionary War and two devastating fires in 1802 and 1855. The building has served as the first capitol of New Jersey, a British garrison prior to the Battle of Princeton in 1777, and the site of the nation's capital when the Continental Congress met there between June and November of 1783. Today it is used for administrative offices, including the President's office.

Paul Robeson's House

110 Witherspoon St., at the corner of Green St., Princeton

Hours: Not open to the public

Paul Robeson is best known as a singer, actor, athlete, and activist.

Princeton Battlefield State Park

Mercer Street, Princeton

Phone: (609) 921-0074

A popular park for picnickers and stargazers, the 85-acre park marks the location of the Battle of Princeton, which was fought in January of 1777 and proved to be a decisive victory for General George Washington and his troops. Located in the park are the Thomas Clark House where General Hugh Mercer died following the Battle of Princeton and the Battle Monument, a depiction of General Washington leading his troops into battle.

Princeton Cemetery

Witherspoon St. and Wiggins St., Princeton

Phone: (609) 924-1639

Leaflets can be obtained from the superintendent's house on Greenview Ave., off Wiggins St., at the entrance to the cemetery. Princeton Cemetery has the graves of Grover Cleveland, Paul Tulane, Henry Van Dyke, Aaron Burr (father and son), John Witherspoon, and Jonathan Edwards.

Rockingham, General Washington's headquarters

Route 518 and River Rd., Rocky Hill

Phone: (609) 921-8835

Hours: Usually open Wednesday-Saturday, 10 a.m.-4 p.m., Sunday, 1 p.m.-4 p.m.

While Congress convened at Nassau Hall, George and Martha Washington lived at Rockingham. In the Blue Room on the second floor, Washington composed his "Farewell Address to the Armies."

University Chapel (1928)

Adjacent to Firestone Library, Princeton University

Free pamphlets are available on site.

Designed by the renowned Gothic Revival architect Ralph Adams Cram, the chapel is 249 feet long, 61 feet wide, and seats 1800 people. Italian stonemasons, working for the Matthews Construction Company, used Pennsylvania sandstone trimmed with Indiana limestone to construct the building. The woodwork was carved from pollard oak imported from England.

Westland, Grover Cleveland's house (1854)

15 Hodge Rd., Princeton

Hours: Not open to the public.

Following his second presidential term, Grover Cleveland moved with his wife to this Georgian Revival house, which they called Westland after Andrew Fleming West, first dean of the Graduate College. In turn, the main tower of the Graduate College was named after Cleveland. Grover Cleveland lived here from 1896 until his death in 1908.

Tours:

The Art Museum

Phone: (609) 258-3787

Point of departure: Museum entrance, McCormick Hall

Departure time: Saturday, 2 p.m.

Orange Key Tours, one-hour tours of the campus

Phone: (609) 258-3603

Point of departure: Frist Campus Center Welcome Desk, 1st floor, Princeton University

Departure times: Monday-Saturday, 10 a.m., 11 a.m., 1:30 p.m., 3:30 p.m., Sunday 1:30 p.m., 3:30 p.m.

Self-Guided Tour of Historic Princeton

Free, Available at Bainbridge House.

Includes places of interest within easy walking distance of the center of town, particularly Princeton's main historic sites.

Small Town, Distinguished Architects

Free, Available at Bainbridge House.

Maps walking tour to buildings designed by some of the country's leading architects. Famed architects include Benjamin Latrobe, Ralph Adams Cram, McKim, Mead & White, and Robert Venturi.

Sunday Walking Tour

Phone: (609) 921-6748

Point of departure: In front of Bainbridge House, 158 Nassau St.

Departure time: Sunday, 2 p.m.

Price: $6 per person, Children under 5 free, Children 6-12 $3, Senior citizens $4

A 1.9-mile guided walking tour of Princeton. Allow 2 hours.

Major Sports Teams:

Philadelphia Phillies (baseball)

New York Yankees (baseball)

New York Mets (baseball)

New Jersey Nets (basketball)

New York Knicks (basketball)

New York Rangers (hockey)

New Jersey Devils (hockey)

Philadelphia Flyers (hockey)

Closest Shopping Malls or Plazas:

Princeton Shopping Center

Market Fair

Princeton Forrestal Village

Quakerbridge Mall

Closest Movie Theatres:

Creative Entertainment Princeton Garden Theatre

160 Nassau St., Princeton Phone: (609) 683-7595

United Artists Movies at Market Fair

3521 US Route 1, PrincetonPhone: (609) 520-8700

AMC Theatres Hamilton 24

325 Sloan Ave., HamiltonPhone: (609) 890-8307

National Amusements Multiplex Cinemas @ Towne Center Plaza

319 Route 130 North, East Windsor
Phone: (609) 371-8470

Students Speak Out On...
Local Atmosphere

"Princeton is a pretty, quiet, and wealthy town, but there isn't a great deal of interaction between school and town. If you want to do a lot of stuff, you can always hop the train to New York City. Manhattan and Philly are an hour away."

"Nassau Street, the main street through the town of Princeton, is **home to many essentially Princeton businesses**. Hoagie Haven, a takeout sandwich shop, stays open late and is to Princeton as the Soup Nazi is to *Seinfeld*. You must know your order before entering the store, and you should try to be in and out as quickly as possible. The owner, George, a campus fixture largely because of his signature mustache, will always take a moment for a quick chat and is very popular amongst students because of his reasonable prices."

"It's a nice town. **It's quiet**, and it has good shopping if you prefer pricier stores and trendy fashions. The town people do not seem to be a problem. It's rather safe as well."

"It's a fairly small town. **Most things are done either on campus or nearby**; you have to drive at least 15 minutes to find stuff away from campus. There is a nice town center at Nassau Street and Palmer Square with lots of shops and restaurants. There's also a movie theater right at the edge of campus. Philly and New York are pretty close, too."

Q "The town of Princeton is **quaint but international**, picturesque but pricey. The seminary school and choir college nearby go more or less unnoticed by undergraduates."

Q "**New Jersey is the heart of everything** in the sense that, from where you will be, you are an hour and a half from the beach, two hours from Atlantic City, three hours from D.C., and 30 minutes from Trenton."

Q "It's a nice atmosphere. **There's a big main street with shops and stores right on campus,** but it's still a small town setting. The people here are extremely friendly."

Q "No student should pass through Princeton without a cappuccino from Small World Coffee, **the heart and soul of the town** and true north of the student body."

Q "Rutgers University and the College of New Jersey are the closest other schools, but **we really don't have anything to do with them.** The town, itself, is very quaint and community-oriented. There are lots of little stores and restaurants, and the campus is one of the most beautiful places I've been to. The architecture and greenery is really breathtaking, especially in the spring and fall."

Q "Princeton's a **quaint little town.** The only other nearby university is Westminster Choir College. The good thing is that Penn Station is only an hour and a half away by train, and a round-trip train ticket is only $14. Plus, there's even a train station on campus."

Q "The **town and university are fairly separate entities**, but the town is small enough that most errands can be done conveniently on foot. The towpath that runs by Lake Carnegie is beautiful. There are some great (but pricey) restaurants."

The College Prowler Take On...
Local Atmosphere

Princeton, New Jersey is a small town with a rich history. Originally the College of New Jersey, Princeton started as a small colonial town centered around a university whose primary focus was to produce well-trained young men, mostly as Presbyterian ministers. Nassau Hall, which now serves as an administrative building, originally housed all of the students, professors, and academic space. With the coming of the American Revolution, it became home to the First Continental Congress. Many legends exist regarding how Nassau Hall received its cannonball blow, a scar that exists even today, reminding students of their importance of their institution in the development of the nation. A walk through the Trustees' Room, which brags a famous Peale portrait of George Washington, also serves as a reminder of Princeton's strong ties with the past, as portraits of every University president hang on the wall.

Many students complain that Princeton is trapped in time essentially because of its older buildings and small town atmosphere. Students looking for an urban campus are sorely mistaken when they arrive on campus by way of the "Dinky," the two-car train that connects Princeton to the main New Jersey Transit rail connection. Princeton undergraduates are generally well received by "townies," but there have been recent tensions between students and local authorities because of proposed changes to the town's alcohol policy. Each year, to help mend any bruised relations, town and gown come together for "Communiversity," a day-long street fair that invites both students and townies to enjoy the closed-off Nassau Street and participate in activities such as a 5K run and sidewalk drawing. Despite its rich history, the university leaves much to be desired by way of a varied social life, so students are forcedto look elsewhere to other places, such as New York and Atlantic City, for a little excitement.

The College Prowler™ Grade on
Local
Atmosphere: C+

A high Local Atmosphere grade indicates that the area surrounding campus is safe and scenic. Other factors include nearby attractions, proximity to other schools, and the town's attitude toward students

Safety & Security

The Lowdown On...
Safety & Security

Number of Princeton University Police:
57

Phone:
911 (emergencies),
(609) 258-3134
(non-emergencies)

Safety Services:
Rape Aggression Defense System (RAD), Bike Registration, Bike Lock Program, Operation I.D., Escort Service, Emergency Phones, Campus Shuttle Service, Assault Prevention Education, Laptop Registration

Health Services:

Clinical Services--Outpatient Services, Inpatient Services, Sexuality Education Counseling and Health Office (annual exams for women including breast and pelvic exams, care for infections and STDs, "morning after pills," preconception advising, pregnancy testing and options, HIV and STD testing, discounted contraception), Allergy Clinic, Immunization Services, Athletic Medicine, TravelSmart Program Counseling Center--Individual & Group Counseling, Sexual Harassment/Assault Resources and Education Program, Eating Concerns Counseling, Alcohol and Other Drugs Counseling

Health Center Office Hours:

Monday, Wednesday, Thursday, Friday, 9 a.m.-4:30 p.m., Tuesday 10 a.m.-4:30 p.m.; Open at all times for emergencies

Did You Know?
Historically, Princeton has had the **lowest campus crime rate in the Ivy League**.

Lyle Menendez was initially rejected from Princeton in 1987 but later gained admission to Princeton's Class of 1991. During his first semester at Princeton, Menendez supposedly received a one-year suspension for plagiarizing a classmate's psychology lab report. After returning to Princeton, Menendez subsequently was placed both on academic and disciplinary probation and was convicted of murdering his parents before he could graduate from Princeton.

Students Speak Out On...
Safety & Security

"There's not much to worry about in terms of safety. There are occasional thefts, but common sense (like locking your door) is enough to prevent it. The biggest risk is getting an expensive bike stolen. Princeton is a small town, and the University is fairly isolated."

Q "Campus **security is very good**. I would have to walk late at night from the library to my dorm, and I had no problems. Public safety was open 24/7, so if you ever needed to call them for any reason, they were available. The Princeton town is pretty small and very safe, so I never had to worry."

Q "I feel very safe on campus. The only time I worry about my safety is sometimes when **I walk back from the student parking lot by myself at night.** There are not many blue phones in depths of the parking lot, so I always make sure to use my cell phone. Sometimes when the weather is bad, I consider using a campus shuttle, but I know I am just letting my imagination wander too much."

Q "The campus is pretty safe. **It is a pretty isolated campus in a small town**, so there really isn't any danger to walking around at night. There are a few instances of people being followed, but these are pretty rare. The school is very responsive to safety. We have Public Safety officers and a lot of phones on campus that you can use to call for help. We used to have rows of bushes by the tennis courts, but these were cut down because people could hide in there and attack people walking by."

Q "I felt secure walking around by myself (as a female, at that) at any hour of the day. **Don't wander to the outer edges right off-campus**, however. They tend to be darker and less secure."

Q "Princeton is very safe. There are people called proctors who make sure everything's going okay. **The building doors all lock automatically** and can only be opened by Princeton students with their ID cards. Campus security is there, but they stay out of our way ... it's good for keeping outsiders away, though."

Q "Our ID cards, or **prox cards, that let us into buildings are overrated.** They are probably more of a scare tactic than anything. You can almost always get someone to let you in if you forget your prox in your room, and if you are persistent enough, you can usually pull the doors open."

Q "**Security and safety are very good.** There's no rampant crime of any kind, with the possible exception of bicycle theft. As long as you always lock your bike, you should be safe from that. I feel safe walking across campus at 5AM. Princeton is a very safe campus; it is arguably the safest you will encounter in the nation. Students can go around campus at any hour without fearing some sort of criminal encounter. I have gone running at 4AM, and I am a girl."

Q "If anything, **Public Safety has too much of a presence on campus.** As long as you use common sense and stay out of certain parts of town by yourself after dark, there is nothing to worry about."

Q "The one piece of advice I would offer about campus safety is to **buy a lock for your laptop and bike.** Also, don't take anything you like too much out to the Street with you. I lock my laptop and bike and have been lucky with both, but I have had four or five jackets taken out at the eating clubs. There's not much you can do about lost jackets except post notices in coat rooms, and don't expect to see lost possessions again."

The College Prowler Take On...
Safety & Security

Princeton has 24-hour campus security. Whether they're breaking up a noisy room party or assisting in medical emergencies, safety officers always pose a strong presence. Because of Princeton's size as both a town and university, most students feel safe enough to walk across campus alone in the middle of the night to the 24-hour WaWa convenience store for a cup of coffee or wrap sandwich after everything else is closed. The most common crime seems to be theft of unattended items, namely laptop computers, bicycles, and jackets. Recently, however, there has been more attention placed on campus sexual violence in the form of date rape thanks to an intensive Take Back the Night program initiated by the Organization for Women Leaders (OWL), a women's issues group founded by several members of Princeton's Class of 2003.

As a town, Princeton is extremely safe. The fact that students feel comfortable walking home from the library rather than constantly worrying about how to get from place to place means that students really have time to concentrate on their studies. Some may even lament that the constant presence of Public Safety officers makes it difficult to have too much fun on campus, but the University has made personal safety a to priority, particularly through the installation of a personal I.D. system for getting into dormitories and other major University Buildings.

The College Prowler™ Grade on

Safety &
Security: A

A high grade in Safety & Security means that students generally feel safe, campus police are visible, blue light phones and escort services are readily available, and safety precautions are not overly necessary.

Computers

The Lowdown On...
Computers

High-Speed Network?
Yes

Wireless Network?
Yes

Number of Labs:
36

Numbers of Computers:
254

Operating Systems:
Windows 95/98/NT/2000/XP,
Macintosh OS, Unix, PUCC

Charge to Print?
No

Free Software:

Norton AntiVirus, Outlook Express, Microsoft Office, Microsoft Internet Explorer, Aladdin (Stuffit) Expander, Adobe Acrobat Reader, RealPlayer

Discounted Software:

Adobe Acrobat, After Effects, Illustrator, InDesign, PageMaker, PhotoShop; CorelDraw Graphics Suite, Vector Effects; FileMaker Pro; Macromedia Dreamweaver MX, Fireworks MX, Flash MX, Freehand MX, ColdFusion MX Developer and Flash Player 6; Microsoft Office 10; Norton SystemWorks

24-Hour Labs:

1942 Hall Basement, Butler Apartments, Carl A. Fields Center Basement, OIT Computing Center, Edwards Hall Basement, 21/22 Forbes College, Gauss Hall Basement, B-9-B Graduate College, Hibben-Magie Apartments, 106 Lawrence Apartments, Lower Madison Hall Common Room, B59 McCosh Hall, McDonnell Hall's Brush Gallery, 33/34 New Graduate College, Julian Street Library

Did You Know?

Princeton's Student Computer Initiative offers discounted desktop and laptop computers, both Windows and Mac, to students. Each student can take advantage of the prices once during his or her four years at Princeton.

Princeton's Department of Public Safety offers laptop registration in an effort to curb the rampant computer theft of the past few years.

The Office of Information Technology (OIT) offers "H-Drive" access to students so that undergraduates can access their files from any computer on the campus network.

Students Speak Out On...
Computers

{ **"Definitely bring your own computer, but there are lots of computer facilities around campus. It only gets really crowded around exam time and around JP and thesis due dates."**

Q "The **computer facilities are very good.** They all have high-speed internet connections and loads of applications. In the new engineering building, there is even a classroom with laptops on every desk. Around midterms and towards the end of the semester, the computer clusters can get pretty crowded with everyone trying to finish the papers. You pretty much need your own computer. Because everyone lives on campus all four years, all rooms have Ethernet. Libraries also have Ethernet outlets so you can bring your laptop and work there. The school offers some subsidized deal to buy computer equipment, and pretty much everyone has there own computer. If not, you can still get by."

Q "Princeton's **very well-connected** and has numerous labs. A computer is actually not needed do the resources, but it does get crowded near finals and midterms. Bring a computer if you can; it makes things easier. For the most part, though, everything is accessible."

Q "Computer clusters **aren't always crowded**, but everyone I knew had their own computer simply because you are almost always writing papers, writing up problem sets, e-mailing or researching. You just spend a lot of time on the computer, so I would really recommend you bring your own—it's certainly more convenient, but the clusters are also available."

Q "I had my own computer and appreciated it, but **you don't need a printer since there are plenty of networked printers.** Lots of people make it through fine without owning a computer. It's probably personal preference, but you might also want to ask current students and check out the web page for more info."

Q "I had my own laptop, but **there were always computers available** in the computer clusters. Internet access is also really fast."

Q "Every room is hardwired for internet access with a T1 connection. As for the computer clusters, **they usually aren't that crowded**, except maybe at finals time when everyone tries to write their papers at once on the last day. Many students bring their own computers, which leaves the rather nice computer clusters unused most of the time."

Q "With its own technology office, **the University invests a lot of money and time in the quality of its computer facilities.** Most buildings have some form of computer cluster or print station, and a campus media lab allows students to go and learn how to use electronics, such as a digital camcorder, to enhance their work."

Q "The school has a computer initiative where **you can buy a subsidized computer.** Desktops are about $800 and laptops are about $1500. But, you can definitely get by without a computer. There are lots of computer clusters, and if you go to the main library, you can borrow a laptop whenever you need one (it just has to stay within the library). The clusters can get crowded towards the end of the semester, just before finals, when all the papers are due, but other than that, it's not a problem. It's just a bit inconvenient during finals."

The College Prowler Take On...
Computers

One of my friend's professors started his first lecture by saying, "Princeton students have the worldwide reputation of being both voracious readers and avid writers." Then, he proceeded to assign several thousand pages of reading for the semester in addition to three papers and a final exam. While this course is definitely the exception rather than the rule, I use it to emphasize the role of Princeton's workload on the average student's daily life. In my senior year alone, I submitted over 250 typed pages of original work, including my senior thesis. To complete this work, my laptop and I spent many hours together in my carrel working. I printed over 700 pages to campus printers, free-of-charge, and read many reserve readings on my laptop in the privacy of my dorm room rather than wait in line in the library's Reserve Room.

The University provides students with access to 24-hour computer support resources, including residential computer consultants who live in the dorms and are able to help students work out computer problems, such as a virus, before they have to bring their computers to a technician. Princeton even has a computer initiative that makes both laptop and desktop computers more affordable to students. For students who opt not to bring a computer, however, all hope is not lost. There are 24-hour computer clusters all over campus. Generally, the computer labs are not crowded except around major deadlines, such as the infamous "Dean's Date," the deadline at the end of the semester for all written work. Some students will hide in the clusters during these intense periods leaving only to eat and shower. For normal assignments, the cluster computers are more than adequate. Students can even save work to a personal, password-protected network drive, which allows them to work on different computers across campus. Short of giving computers away to students, it is hard to believe that the University's computer system could get much better.

A-

The College Prowler™ Grade on

Computers: A-

A high grade in Computers designates that computer labs are available, the computer network is easily accessible, and the campus' computing technology is up to date.

Facilities

The Lowdown On...
Facilities

Student Center:
Frist Campus Center

Campus Size:
500 acres

Athletic Center:
Dillon Gym (Stephens Fitness
Center, Dillon Pool, Squash
Courts)
DeNunzio Pool
Pagoda Tennis Courts
Jadwin Gym

Popular Places to Chill
Café Vivian
1903 Courtyard
Wilson Courtyard
Frist Dining Level

Libraries:
19

Favorite Things to Do:

Princeton students are avid sports fans, so football, basketball, ice hockey, and lacrosse games tend to draw huge student contingents. The new Frist Campus Center is a popular place, as it houses an extensive dining facility, the campus coffeehouse Café Vivian, the campus movie theater, and vast classroom space. In addition to the performance space in Frist, many campus performance spaces are used on almost a weekly basis for the various dance groups, acting troupes, and a cappella groups on campus.

What Is There to Do?

Without even leaving campus, students can take a run around Carnegie Lake, go to a movie for $2, watch excellent live theater including the famous Triangle Club kick line (of cross-dressing men), work out in the state-of-the-art gym facilities, practice their musical instruments or have a music lesson, develop photos in one of several campus dark rooms, or sip a latte in the Campus Center's Café Vivian, which is named for the wife of former University President Harold Shapiro.

Movie Theatre on Campus?

Yes. Frist Campus Center Film/Performance Theatre, Frist Campus Center.

Bowling on Campus?

No.

Bar on Campus?

No.

Coffeehouse on Campus?

Yes. Café Vivian, Frist Campus Center.

"Most facilities are excellent, and there are lots of new buildings, centers, libraries, etc. The new student center is excellent and gives a reasonable alternative to dining halls."

Q "The main athletic facility for non-varsity athletes is Dillon gym. It is pretty old … but there are four basketball courts, two aerobics rooms, and a brand new fitness center, so I guess it's okay. There are computer clusters located all over campus that are very nice. The student center is only a couple of years old, so it is also pretty nice—it's becoming **a place for people to eat, hang out, and study.** The classrooms are okay as well."

Q "There was a new engineering building finished this year, the Friend Center, and its classrooms all have projection TVs with the latest audio/video equipment as well as some really nice chairs. **The older classrooms are pretty standard.**"

Q "**They are the best!** Everything is as perfect as can be in that regard. I fell in love with Princeton the moment I saw it. We have a new student center, which is supposed to be one of the best in the nation."

Q "The **gym is really crowded during certain times of the day**—right after classes let out, dinner-time, especially just before closing. The best thing to do is to go in between classes or right at opening."

Q "They're great. **Princeton just got a new track two years ago**, and the student center was remodeled and looks great! Everything is excellent. There's a new gym fitness room, new computers, and nice housing. The old buildings are all fixed up, and there are a lot of new buildings. They are all kept clean and safe, and there is a lot of history to them."

Q "The **Frist Student Center can get really crowded**, especially during exams. The third floor study room used to be a fantastic refuge for those seeking silence, but people have started to bring in Discmen and food and camp out for what seems like days. If you're looking for a good place to study in Frist now, it is a good idea to seek out an empty classroom or go next door to the East Asian Library."

Q "The facilities at the new Friend Center are great. The building has those chairs that cost something ridiculous like $800. **You can almost always find a good, quiet place to work**, and it is close enough to the eating clubs, so it is great for upperclassmen who can easily break for lunch or dinner."

Q "**They just redid the gym**, so it's really nice now. There's also another gym for athletes. Right now, they're in the process of a 20-year dorm renovation, where they take one dorm each year and completely redo it. I think Princeton is the richest school in the country, so they definitely have the money to provide the finest facilities."

Q "**Café Viv was really nice when it first opened.** It was never too crowded. Now, even with a larger staff, people are always there, so it is not always the best place to study."

Q "They're pretty darn good. **They're first-rate** and are kept in good shape, too—partly because the University has money out the kazoo, and partly because vandalism isn't much of an issue. The new exercise center in Dillon Gym is amazing."

Q "Some of Princeton's dorms are **downright nasty.** It's nice that they're redoing them over the next twenty years, but most of the toilet and shower stalls have shower curtains instead of doors."

Q "The newly renovated **Marquand Library is phenomenal**. The study carrels are huge, and the building is in the middle of campus. Art history majors can't ask for more in their library."

The College Prowler Take On...
Facilities

Common student facilities, such as the gym and student center, are state-of-the-art. The student gym, Stephens Fitness Center in Dillon Gym, was recently renovated and the machines updated, but the biggest problem in the minds of the vastly health-conscious students is how long the wait is for a treadmill or elliptical machine. The student government continues to battle with the issue of gym overpopulation, and machines are added to the limited space on a regular basis. The Frist Campus Center opened in 2000, increasing student space dramatically. Students now have a campus coffee shop, convenience store, food court, and smoothie stand where they can charge everything to their student account, much to the chagrin of many Princeton parents suffering from the phenomenon known as "Frist sticker shock."

Princeton has made a lot of recent strides to catch up with other major universities in terms of campus facilities. Until 2000, students were forced to cram into the small but character-filled Chancellor Green, which was recently renovated and now has a gorgeous reading room in the rotunda. Perhaps it was poor planning or just not realizing how popular new facilities would be, but Frist Campus Center and Stephens Fitness Center both face overcrowding problems, which will only get worse as the University expands its student body.

The College Prowler™ Grade on

Facilities: B+

A high Facilities grade indicates that the campus is aesthetically pleasing and well maintained, facilities are state-of-the-art, and libraries are exceptional. Other determining factors include the quality of both athletic and student centers and an abundance of things to do on campus.

Campus Dining

The Lowdown On...
Campus Dining

Freshman Meal Plan Requirement?

Yes

Meal Plan Average Cost:

$3,816

Places to Grab a Bite with Your Meal Plan:

Butler College Dining Hall

Location: Wu Hall

Food: Basic dining hall fare—hot line, grill, salad bar, fruit basket, dessert bar, sandwich bar, frozen yogurt

Favorite Dish: Breaded chicken stuffed with broccoli and cheese

Hours: Monday-Friday, 7:30 a.m.-10 a.m., 11:30 a.m.-1:30 p.m., 5:30 p.m.-7:30 p.m., Saturday 10 a.m.-1:30 p.m., 5:30 p.m.-7:30 p.m., Sunday 11 a.m.-1:30 p.m., 5:30 p.m.-7:30 p.m.

Deli

Location: Frist Campus Center

Food: Salads and sandwiches

Favorite Dish: Build-your-own salad

Hours: Check http://facilities. princeton.edu/dining/_Frist_ Dining/ for schedule.

Food for Thought

Location: Frist Campus Center

Food: Comfort food

Favorite Dish: Roasted chicken with creamed spinach and macaroni and cheese

Hours: Check http://facilities. princeton.edu/dining/_Frist_ Dining/ for schedule.

Forbes College Dining Hall

Location: Main Inn, Forbes College

Food: Basic dining hall fare— hot line, grill, salad bar, fruit basket, dessert bar, sandwich bar, frozen yogurt

Favorite Dish: Sunday brunch buffet including bagels and lox

Hours: Monday-Friday 7:30 a.m.-10 a.m., 11:30 a.m.-1:30 p.m., 5:30 p.m.-7:30 p.m., Saturday 10 a.m.-1:30 p.m., 5:30 p.m.-7:30 p.m., Sunday 11 a.m.-1:30 p.m., 5:30 p.m.- 7:30 p.m.

The Grill

Location: Frist Campus Center

Food: Fast food, Mongolian Grill

Favorite Dish: Stir fry chicken with noodles

Hours: Check http://facilities. princeton.edu/dining/_Frist_ Dining/ for schedule.

Mathey College Dining Hall

Location: Madison Hall

Food: Basic dining hall fare— hot line, grill, salad bar, fruit basket, dessert bar, sandwich bar, frozen yogurt

Favorite Dish: Chicken fajitas

Hours: Monday-Friday, 7:30 a.m.-10 a.m., 11:30 a.m.-1:30 p.m., 5:30 p.m.-7:30 p.m., Saturday 10 a.m.-1:30 p.m., 5:30 p.m.-7:30 p.m., Sunday 11 a.m.-1:30 p.m., 5:30 p.m.- 7:30 p.m.

Rockefeller "Rocky" College Dining Hall

Location: Holder Hall

Food: Basic dining hall fare— hot line, grill, salad bar, fruit basket, dessert bar, sandwich bar, frozen yogurt

Favorite Dish: Grilled cheese with French fries

Hours: Monday-Friday, 7:30 a.m.-10 a.m., 11:30 a.m.-1:30 p.m., 5:30 p.m.-7:30 p.m., Saturday 10 a.m.-1:30 p.m., 5:30 p.m.-7:30 p.m., Sunday 11 a.m.-1:30 p.m., 5:30 p.m.- 7:30 p.m.

Villa Pizza

Location: Frist Campus Center

Food: Pizza and pasta

Favorite Dish: Deep dish meat lovers' pizza

Hours: Check http://facilities. princeton.edu/dining/_Frist_ Dining/ for schedule.

Wilson College Dining Hall

Location: Wilcox Hall

Food: Basic dining hall fare— hot line, grill, salad bar, fruit basket, dessert bar, sandwich bar, frozen yogurt

Favorite Dish: Shrimp and Scallop Stir-fry

Hours: Monday-Friday, 7:30 a.m.-10 a.m., 11:30 a.m.-1:30 p.m., 5:30 p.m.-7:30 p.m., Saturday 10 a.m.-1:30 p.m., 5:30 p.m.-7:30 p.m., Sunday 11 a.m.-1:30 p.m., 5:30 p.m.- 7:30 p.m.

24-Hour On-Campus Eating?

No

Student Favorites:

Forbes College Dining Hall, The Grill, Villa Pizza, Deli

Other Options:

After sophomore year, most students elect to move out of their residential colleges, forfeit their meal plan option, and move into upperclass housing. In upperclass housing, students must decide whether they want to join an eating club, one of the campus co-ops, or "go independent." For those who go independent, they have the option to move into Spelman Hall, a group of dormitory buildings designed by I.M. Pei, which contains suites of four singles, a kitchen, bathroom, and common room. This is also where the married students live. There are two campus co-ops— 2D, a vegetarian co-op, and Brown, named for its kitchen in Brown Hall.

The majority of students opt not to cook for themselves and join co-ed eating clubs. There are eleven active eating clubs on Prospect Avenue, or "The Street." To join an eating club, students must decide whether they want to "bicker" or "sign-in" at the start of the second semester of their sophomore year.

There are five bicker clubs, and to gain membership, students must participate in what is essentially a three day rush period. Once a student decides to bicker, he or she can only bicker a single club. Bicker process varies by club, and there are often concerns of the rights of female students during bicker, but clubs try to keep the process as clean as possible. Some clubs conduct interviews of the bickering sophomores while other bicker processes resemble the physical challenge from Nickelodeon's old show "Double Dare." At the end of bicker, members of the club conduct extensive discussions on each of the sophomores. Once that process is complete and the new bicker class has been selected, members of the club run around campus picking up the new members. The next night, each bicker club holds a secretive initiations ceremony.

Sign in clubs have open membership, and students have two opportunities to sign in. The first chance comes before bicker even begins. A group of up to eight students, male and female, fills out a form with their top three club choices. The Inter-Club Council then holds a random lottery to see which groups will go into each of the clubs. Typically, only one or two of the sign in clubs will fill in this first round process. After sophomores are notified that evening of the results of their sign in, members of the sign ins clubs go and pick up the new sophomores much like the bicker clubs do later in the week. The sign in clubs then host a week of parties for the new members so that they can learn club tradition and meet some of the older members. Because most of the sign in clubs do not fill during the first round, a second round is held after the results of bicker come in so that students who bickered and did not receive an invitation are given the chance to join a club. Another random lottery is held and the results of the second lottery are announced the day of bicker club initiations. Sign in clubs hold their secretive initiations on different nights, but they make sure that the second round sign in sophomores feel just as welcome as anyone else in the club through events in the following weeks like semi-formals and members-only dinners.

Sophomores do not have the full privileges of membership until their junior year. They do, however, have to pay a one-time initiation fee, which usually goes to cover the cost of spring-time events at the clubs. The dues at each of the clubs vary. Bicker clubs are generally more expensive than sign-in clubs with annual dues of around $7,000 rather than $5,500. Both types of clubs provide breakfast, lunch, and dinner during the week and brunch and dinner over the weekend. In addition to meals, each of the clubs provide a club house for members to use. Again, the facilities vary by club, but each club generally contains an underground taproom, residential space for club officers, a dining room, a dance floor, a TV room, and a computer cluster.

All of the clubs host a fall Lawnparties the first weekend after fall semester classes start, a winter formal the last weekend before fall classes end, and spring Houseparties the weekend after spring semester classes end. Other than that, the social activities at each club vary from weekly DJ parties to live concerts. Some clubs join with other clubs to promote better club relations hosting events such as the Cottage-Ivy New York Bar Night. Generally, as long as you are in a club with your friends and can afford the luxury of joining an eating club, it is one of Princeton's best social institutions. While bicker may cause some great disappointments, the food at the eating clubs is great, and the lack of nearby groceries and alternative social options makes the independent life at Princeton even more difficult at times.

Did You Know?

Princeton's Dining Services won a prestigious Ivy Award with five other groups, including **the famous New York sushi institution Nobu**.

Students with a meal plan may request to **organize a cookout**, and all food and supplies are available at the contract holders' dining unit.

Students may request a **bagged lunch** in the Dining Hall at breakfast if they are going to miss lunch.

From Monday breakfast through Friday lunch, students who miss a meal in the dining halls are able to use their meals at the **Frist Campus Center Food Galley**.

Students with a meal plan can eat in one of the eating clubs under **a Meal Exchange program**. Once the contract holder has a meal in the eating club, the eating club member must have the same meal in the dining hall.

Sledding anyone? With the uncharacteristic snowfalls of the 2002-2003 academic year, students "borrowed" trays from Frist to go **sledding on the hills of the golf course** behind Forbes College.

Once a semester, Dining Services organizes to have a local restaurant come to each of the residential colleges and **cook a gourmet meal**. Recent cuisines have ranged from Ethiopian to French.

Students Speak Out On...
Campus Dining

{ **"The food is pretty good; the student center has excellent options. Plus, the upperclassmen 'eating clubs' have very good food as well."**

Q "For the first two years **students live and eat in Residential Colleges.** The food at the colleges varies greatly, with Rockefeller being one of the worst and Forbes being the best. Students have some flexibility because any underclassman on the meal plan can eat at any of the dining halls. Location tends to be a factor, however, as Forbes in particular is far away from the center of campus."

Q "Although **the dining hall is a good place to socialize** when you first get to school, it won't necessarily provide the best meals. Most of the food consists of pre-made dishes with colorful names such as 'Calypso Pork.' Upperclassmen are able to join one of the eating clubs. The food at the clubs is better than the food at dining halls and also tends to vary. Some clubs, such as Terrace, regularly provide a vegetarian option while the Cottage Club is known for its steak nights and a glut of salmon dishes."

Q "Students who decide not to join a club declare themselves 'independent' and become responsible for finding and cooking all of their meals. **Independence is doable, especially if you have a car** or draw into a room with a kitchen. Many independent students are able to get by eating at local restaurants and at the student center."

Q "The food is **pretty good;** the student center has excellent options. Plus, the upperclassmen 'eating clubs' have very good food as well."

Q "I can't say that it's gourmet dining, but **I have no real complaints.**"

Q **"Food is generally very average.** It's your basic dining hall buffet food; we got sick of it pretty quickly. At the end of sophomore year, you join an eating club. There are 10 eating clubs on Prospect Street ('The Street'); they are where you will eat your meals and hang out. It's similar to a frat, I guess. The food at eating clubs is generally much better than the dining halls. The club I was in, Charter, probably had the best food on the street. We had pub nights two times a week, with international food on Wednesdays. All in all, the food was very good, although lunches could be mediocre. People who don't join eating clubs are independent and have to cook for themselves."

Q "The food is good.... **The dining halls have a huge selection**, and the Frist Campus Center is awesome. Meal times are a really good time to hang out with friends."

Q "The food in the dining halls is **pretty good.** After graduation, you'll quickly miss the unlimited amounts and varieties of food! This year, I think the food situation has gotten even better, since they built a new student center. Starting junior year, you'll have the option of joining an eating club, which serves fewer people and generally has better food than the dining halls. Depending on the club, you might even have gourmet food."

Q **"Eating clubs do not offer as many dining options as the University-run dining halls**, but the food is generally better, and students spend more time with a smaller group of people, thus making the club system open to stereotypes of exclusivity as perpetuated by classic works such as F. Scott Fitzgerald's *This Side of Paradise*."

Q "Since the new Frist Campus Center opened this year, **the number of food options has greatly increased.** The dining hall food isn't bad, actually, I enjoyed it."

Q "Undergrads usually join eating clubs after their first year—this means expensive dues. **Students who can't afford it have to go around looking for food or eat in the dorms.** There is one 'nontraditional' house where you can get vegetarian health food. The social life is built around the eating clubs, and if you can't afford it, you can be an outsider."

Q "The **dining halls are pretty good for freshman** and sophomores. As you enter your junior year, students have the option of joining an eating club. The food is even better and desserts are always plentiful, which could also be a bad thing if you are not careful."

Q "Initially, students are **split into five residential colleges,** which provides them with a set of dorms, a college staff, and a dining hall. Students may eat in any dining hall on campus, regardless of their own residence. Freshmen and sophomores have to live in their residential college and cannot look for off-campus housing. In the residential colleges, freshmen and sophomores receive academic support and build somewhat of a home for themselves by living closely amongst a fifth of their classmates."

Q "The first two years you have to eat in the dining hall. The food there is okay—**not that great**—but you can always have a hamburger or hot dog made, and there's also always a salad bar and cereal. For your second and third years, you have the option to either join an eating club or go independent and cook for yourself. You could also join a co-op, where everyone pitches in with the cooking. The food in the eating clubs is generally pretty good because the chefs are hired by the students, and fewer people eat in each club in the dining hall."

Q "Each dining hall consists of **a main hot line, a salad bar, a grill, and a cold buffet.** There are always vegetarian options besides the salad bar. The main hot line typically consists of two or three main dinner options. If students do not find something on the main line, they can go to the grill, where they can short order items such as grilled chicken, hamburgers, or grilled cheese. Another option at the grill is the short order dish, "Show Thyme," an item made to order by a member of the kitchen staff, ranging from chicken fajitas to tofu stir-fry. The salad bar offers a wide range of fruits and vegetables, such as spinach and sprouts. There is also fresh fruit, primarily apples, oranges, and bananas, available at all times. Generally, the quality of food in the dining hall is decent, and there are always options."

Q "The dining hall food is **very good, especially compared to a lot of other schools.** Our new campus center has especially good food, although it's slightly more expensive."

Q "Freshmen and sophomores eat in the dining halls. **The food there is slightly better than average college food.** The dining halls' selections are virtually identical for each meal, so it doesn't matter which you go to, although some say that one called Forbes has the best Sunday brunch."

The College Prowler Take On...
Campus Dining

The strength of Princeton's dining hall facilities is that they have many options. While the food in the hot line tends to be somewhat tasteless and boring, although that is changing, events such as the visiting restaurant night more than make up for it. Sunday brunch is by far the best meal of the week, and students are more than willing to struggle out of bed on Sunday mornings to get to the dining halls for made to order omelets and bagels and lox. Eating in the dining halls does get boring after two years, so the vast majority of students opt to go independent, join a co-op, or join an eating club. The food quality at the co-ops and the eating clubs is varied. While some clubs brag award-winning chefs, others complain about a constant barrage of fried foods. The common thread that students enjoy in both the eating clubs and the dining halls is an active social scene, and meal time at Princeton is seen generally more as a social hour than a period of nourishment.

Despite the exciting dining options readily available, they do not come without a huge cost and relative inflexibility in scheduling. The lack of a 24-hour campus dining facility can be frustrating during exam periods, but the University has promised to address that issue in coming months. Furthermore, the costly dues of the eating clubs leave them open to those who can afford it, thus leaving the clubs open to the critique that they are active remnants of Princeton's elitist history. Independents also complain about the high cost of food in the town of Princeton and the dearth of a major grocery store within walking distance. Essentially, Princeton's dining facilities offer many options to students for a price.

The College Prowler™ Grade on
Campus Dining: B+

Our grade on Campus Dining addresses the quality of both school-owned dining halls and independent on campus restaurants as well as the price, availability, and variety of food available.

Off-Campus Dining

The Lowdown On...
Off-Campus Dining

Restaurant Prowler: Popular Places to Eat!

Ajihei
Food: Japanese
Address: 11 Chambers St.
Phone: (609) 252-1158
Price: $25 and under per person
Hours: Daily 6 p.m.-9 p.m.

The Alchemist and Barrister

Food: American
Address: 28 Witherspoon St.
Phone: (609) 924-5555
Cool Features: Includes two dining rooms, casual patio dining area, and traditional pub
Price: $25 and under per person
Hours: Monday-Thursday 11:30 a.m.-10 p.m., Friday-Saturday 11:30 a.m.-10:30 p.m., Sunday 11 a.m.-10 p.m.

→

Annex Restaurant

Food: American

Address: 128 1/2 Nassau St

Phone: (609) 921-7555

Cool Features: Happy hour food and drink specials, Murals of Princeton in bar

Price: $10 and under per person

Hours: Monday-Saturday 11:30 a.m.-12:30 a.m.

Blue Point Grill

Food: Seafood

Address: 258 Nassau St.

Phone: (609) 921-1211

Cool Features: Fish fresh from adjacent Nassau Street Seafood Market

Price: $30 and under per person

Hours: Tuesday-Saturday 5 p.m.-10 p.m., Sunday-Monday 5 p.m.-9 p.m.

Bucks County Coffee Company

Food: Coffee, bakery, sandwiches

Address: 5 Palmer Square West

Phone: (609) 497-6877

Price: $5 and under per person

Hours: Monday-Thursday 7:30 a.m.-10 p.m., Friday-Saturday 7:30 a.m.-11 p.m., Sunday 7:30 a.m.-8 p.m.

Burger King

Food: Fast food

Address: 84 Nassau St.

Phone: (609) 683-9817

Price: $5 and under per person

Hours: Monday-Saturday 6 a.m.-11 p.m., Sunday 6 a.m.-10 p.m.

Carousel Luncheonette

Food: American

Address: 260 Nassau St.

Phone: (609) 924-2677

Price: $10 and under per person

Hours: Sunday-Thursday 6 a.m.-10 p.m., Friday-Saturday 6 a.m.-2 a.m.

Chez Alice

Food: Bakery, salads, sandwiches

Address: 254 Nassau St.

Phone: (609) 921-6707

Price: $10 and under per person

Hours: Monday-Thursday, Saturday 7 a.m.-6 p.m., Friday 7 a.m.-7 p.m., Sunday 7 a.m.-3 p.m.

Chuck's Spring Street Café

Food: American

Address: 16 Spring St.

Phone: (609) 921-0027

Price: $10 and under per person

Hours: Daily 11 a.m.-9:30 p.m.

Cox's Market
Food: Deli
Address: 180 Nassau St.
Phone: (609) 924-6269
Price: $5 and under per person
Hours: Daily 6 a.m.-5 p.m.

The Ferry House
Food: American, French
Address: 32 Witherspoon St.
Phone: (609) 924-2488
Price: $40 and under per person
Hours: Monday-Friday 11:30 a.m.-2:30 p.m., 5 p.m.-10 p.m., Saturday 5 p.m.-10 p.m., Sunday 4 p.m.-9 p.m.

George's Roasters and Ribs
Food: American
Address: 244 Nassau St.
Phone: (609) 252-0419
Price: $10 and under per person
Hours: Monday-Saturday 11 a.m.-11 p.m.

Golden Orchid
Food: Chinese
Address: 238 Nassau St.
Phone: (609) 921-2388
Cool Feature: Outdoor dining offered
Price: $15 and under per person
Hours: Monday-Friday 11:30 a.m.-10 p.m., Saturday 11:30 a.m.-10:30 p.m., Sunday 12 p.m.-9:30 p.m.

Halo Pub
Food: Ice cream, coffee
Address: 9 Hulfish St.
Phone: (609) 921-1710
Price: $5 and under per person
Hours: Sunday-Friday 7 a.m.-11 p.m., Saturday 7 a.m.-11:30 p.m.

Hoagie Haven
Food: Sandwiches
Address: 242 Nassau St.
Phone: (609) 921-7723
Price: $5 and under per person
Hours: Daily 9 a.m.-1 a.m.

Ichiban Japanese Cuisine
Food: Japanese
Address: 66 Witherspoon St.
Phone: (609) 683-8323
Price: $25 and under per person
Hours: Monday-Saturday 11:30 a.m.-10 p.m., Sunday 2:30 p.m.-9:30 p.m.

JB Winberie Restaurant and Bar
Food: American
Address: 1 Palmer Square East, # 1
Phone: (609) 921-0700
Price: $15 and under per person
Hours: Monday-Saturday 11 a.m.-12 a.m., Sunday 10 a.m.-10 p.m.

Kalluri Corner

Food: Indian

Address: 235a Nassau St.

Phone: (609) 688-8923

Price: $20 and under

Hours: Daily 11:30 a.m.-3:30 p.m., 5 p.m.-10:30 p.m.

Karen's Chinese Restaurant

Food: Chinese

Address: 36 Witherspoon St.

Phone: (609) 683-1968

Price: $15 and under

Hours: Monday-Friday 11:30 a.m.-10 p.m., Saturday-Sunday 12 p.m.-10 p.m.

Lahieres Restaurant

Food: Continental, French, American

Address: 5 Witherspoon St.

Phone: (609) 921-2798

Cool Feature: Party room

Price: $50 and under

Hours: Monday-Saturday 11:30 a.m.-2:30 p.m., 5:30 p.m.-10 p.m.

La Mezzaluna

Food: Italian

Address: 25 Witherspoon St.

Phone: (609) 688-8515

Price: $40 and under

Hours: Sunday 5 p.m.-9 p.m., Monday-Thursday 11:30 a.m.-2:30 p.m., 5 p.m.-9 p.m., Friday 11:30 a.m.-2:30 p.m., 5 p.m.-10 p.m., Saturday 5 p.m.-10 p.m.

Les Compains

Food: French

Address: 18 Witherspoon St.

Phone: (609) 683-4771

Price: $40 and under per person

Hours: Monday-Thursday 11:30 a.m.-2 p.m., 5:30 p.m.-9 p.m., Friday 11:30 a.m.-2 p.m., 5:30 p.m.-10 p.m.

Masala Grill

Food: Indian

Address: 15 Chambers St.

Phone: (609) 921-0500

Price: $20 and under per person

Hours: Daily 12 p.m.-3 p.m., 5 p.m.-10 p.m.

Mediterra Restaurant

Food: Continental

Address: 29 Hulfish St.

Phone: (609) 252-9680

Price: $40 and under

Hours: Monday-Thursday 11:30 a.m.-11 p.m., Friday-Saturday 11:30 a.m.-12 a.m., Sunday 12 p.m.-10 p.m.

Moondoggie Café

Food: Sandwiches, Salads

Address: 33 Witherspoon St.

Phone: (609) 252-0300

Cool Features: Student discount

Price: $10 and under per person

Hours: Daily 8 a.m.-7 p.m.

Nassau Bagel and Sushi

Food: Bagels, Japanese

Address: 179 Nassau St.

Phone: (609) 497-3275

Price: Bagels: $5 and under per person, Sushi: $20 and under per person

Hours: Bagels: Daily 6 a.m.-3 p.m., Sushi: Daily 11:30 a.m.-10:30 p.m.

Old World Pizza

Food: Pizza

Address: 242 1/2 Nassau St.

Phone: (609) 924-9321

Price: $10 and under per person

Hours: Monday-Saturday 11 a.m.-10 p.m., Sunday 4 p.m.-9 pm.

Olives

Food: Greek, deli, bakery

Address: 22 Witherspoon St.

Phone: (609) 921-1569

Cool Features: Warm chocolate chip cookies, takeout only

Price: $5 and under per person

Hours: Daily 7 a.m.-7 p.m.

Panera Bread Bakery and Café

Food: Bread, sandwiches, salads, coffee

Address: 136 Nassau St.

Phone: (609) 688-1692

Cool Features: Free coffee refills, free bread samples

Price: $10 and under per person

Hours: Monday-Thursday 6 a.m.-9 p.m., Friday-Saturday 6 a.m.-10 p.m., Sunday 7 a.m.-9 p.m.

PJ's Pancake House

Food: American

Address: 154 Nassau St.

Phone: (609) 924-1353

Price: $10 and under per person

Hours: Sunday-Thursday 6 a.m.-10 p.m., Friday-Saturday 7 a.m.-12 a.m.

Pizza Colore

Food: Pizza

Address: 124 Nassau St.

Phone: (609) 924-0777

Price: $5 and under per person

Hours: Monday-Friday 11 a.m.-10 p.m., Saturday 11 a.m.-11 p.m., Sunday 11 a.m.-9 p.m.

Le Plumet Royal

Food: French

Address: 20 Bayard Lane

Phone: (609) 921-0050

Price: $40 and under per person

Hours: Daily 11:45 a.m.-3 p.m., 5 p.m.-10 p.m.

Red Onion

Food: Deli

Address: 20 Nassau St.

Phone: (609) 924-6667

Price: $5 and under per person

Hours: Daily 6:30 a.m.-4:30 p.m.

Rusty Scupper

Food: American

Address: 378 Alexander St.

Phone: (609) 921-3276

Price: $25 and under per person

Hours: Monday-Thursday 11:30 a.m.-2:30 p.m., 5 p.m.-10 p.m., Friday 11:30 a.m.-2:30 p.m., 5 p.m.-11 p.m., Saturday 5 p.m.-11 p.m., Sunday 2 p.m.-9 p.m.

Sakura Express

Food: Japanese

Address: 43 Witherspoon St.

Phone: (609) 430-1180

Price: $15 and under

Hours: Daily 12 p.m.-2:45 p.m., 4:30 p.m.-9:15 p.m.

Sally Lunn's Tea Shop

Food: English

Address: 164 Nassau St.

Phone: (609) 430-1071

Price: $15 and under per person

Hours: Monday-Friday 10:30 a.m.-5:30 p.m., Saturday-Sunday 10:30 a.m.-6:30 p.m.

Small World Coffee

Food: Café

Address: 14 Witherspoon St.

Phone: (609) 924-4377

Cool Features: Coffee saver card

Price: $5 and under per person

Hours: Monday-Thursday 6:30 a.m.-9:30 p.m., Friday-Saturday 6:30 a.m.-11 p.m., Sunday 7:30 a.m.-9:30 p.m.

Soonja's Café with Sushi

Food: Chinese, Japanese, Thai

Address: 242 Alexander St.

Phone: (609) 924-9260

Price: $15 and under per person

Hours: Monday-Saturday 11:30 a.m.-3 p.m., 5:30 p.m.-10 p.m., Sunday 5 p.m.-10 p.m.

Teresa's Cafe Italiano

Food: Italian

Address: 21 Palmer Square East

Phone: (609) 921-1974

Price: $20 and under per person

Hours: Monday-Thursday 11 a.m.-11 p.m., Friday-Saturday 11 a.m.-12 a.m., Sunday 12 p.m.-10 p.m.

Thai Village

Food: Thai

Address: 235 Nassau St.

Phone: (609) 683-3896

Cool Features: Party room

Price: $15 and under per person

Hours: Monday-Saturday 11:30 a.m.-10 p.m., Sunday 12 p.m.-9:30 p.m.

Thomas Sweet Ice Cream

Food: Ice cream and chocolate

Address: 183 Nassau St.

Phone: (609) 683-8720

Cool Features: Homemade ice cream, Two-for-Tuesday specials during the school year

Price: $5 and under per person

Hours: Sunday-Thursday 11 a.m.-11 p.m., Friday-Saturday 11 a.m.-12 a.m.

Tiger Noodles

Food: Chinese

Address: 260 Nassau St.

Phone: (609) 252-0663

Price: $15 and under per person

Hours: Sunday-Thursday

11:30 a.m.-10 p.m., Friday-Saturday 11:30 a.m.-11:30 p.m.

Tortuga's Mexican Village

Food: Mexican

Address: 42 Leigh Ave.

Phone: (609) 924-5143

Price: $15 and under per person

Triumph Brewing Company

Food: American

Address: 138 Nassau St.

Phone: (609) 924-7855

Cool Features: Frequent live entertainment, tours of the brewery offered

Price: $20 and under per person

Hours: Regular Menu: Monday-Saturday 11:30 a.m.-10 p.m., Sunday 12 p.m.-9 p.m., Abbreviated Menu: Monday-Saturday 10 p.m.-12 a.m., Bar Only: Monday-Wednesday 12 a.m.-1 a.m., Thursday-Saturday 12 a.m.-2 a.m., Sunday 9 p.m.-12 a.m.

Victor's Pizza
Food: Pizza
Address: 86 Nassau St.
Phone: (609) 924-5515
Price: $5 and under per person
Hours: Daily 11 a.m.-11 p.m.

Yankee Doodle Tap Room
Food: American
Address: 10 Palmer Square East
Phone: (609) 921-7500
Price: $25 and under per person
Hours: Daily 11a.m.-10 p.m.

Zorba's Grill
Food: Greek
Address: 183 Nassau St.
Phone: (609) 924-2454
Cool Features: Takeout only
Price: $5 and under per person
Hours: Daily 8 a.m.-8 p.m.

24-Hour Eating:
Wa Wa Food Market

Closest Grocery Store:
Wild Oats Community Market
255 Nassau St.
Phone: (609) 924-4993

Student Favorites:

Annex Restaurant

Golden Orchid

Hoagie Haven

Olives

Panera Bread Bakery and Café

PJ's Pancake House

Sakura Express

Small World Coffee

Teresa's Cafe Italiano

Thai Village

Thomas Sweet Ice Cream

Triumph Brewing Company

Best Pizza:

Old World Pizza

Best Chinese:

Golden Orchid

Best Breakfast:

PJ's Pancake House

Best Wings:

Chuck's Spring Street Café

Best Healthy:

Moondoggie Café

Best Place to Take Your Parents:

The Ferry House

Mediterra Restaurant

Blue Point Grill

Did You Know?

Fun Facts:

With the recent influx of Princeton by sushi restaurants, there are several **"Princeton rolls" and "Tiger rolls" around town**.

Some of the town's seafood restaurants, including **the Blue Point Grill**, have amazingly fresh fish, thanks to Nassau Street Seafood Market, which purchases its fish at the famous Fulton Fish Market in New York.

Students Speak Out On...
Off-Campus Dining

"There are tons of restaurants around—pizza, Italian, Japanese, Chinese, Thai, etc. There are good ones and bad ones; it really depends how much you want to pay."

Q "There are some really nice off-campus restaurants because Princeton is a wealthy town. Some good places to eat include: Teresa's, Thai Village, and Triumph Brewing Company. I didn't eat off campus very much because I'm too cheap and all our meals were provided for us. These restaurants can be pretty pricy at about **$10 - $20 for an entrée.** There are some fast-food places like Burger King, but the best spot is Hoagie Haven—they make subs, hamburgers, and fries, and they make it cheap. It's open late, and it's near the engineering building; a lot of students swing by if they're working late at night."

Q "The **restaurants are very good,** but they're a little pricey due to the demographics of the Princeton area. For economy-style dining, Hoagie Haven and the WaWa convenience store are both very good. There are also good Asian selections."

Q "Blue Point Grill and Ajihei are the best for seafood and sushi, respectively. **The Ferry House is also incredible for seafood.**"

Q **"It's so good! Mmmm** ... Thai Village is so yummy and cheap. Teresa's is so good (Italian, pizzas, stuff), and Orchid Pavilion has yummy Chinese. There is really anything you want from sushi to American. It is all so yummy!"

Q "The Annex is a bar and restaurant located on Nassau Street across from the main library. **Also reasonably priced, the Annex becomes a popular haunt for seniors** who will leave the library and the dreaded senior thesis only for last call, which coincides with the closing of the library."

Q "There are **some good places very near the campus** within easy walking distance. The favorite is a place called Hoagie Haven—they've got over 50 kinds of hoagies that are all very good and cheap. There are plenty of $25-a-plate places, but there are also some other good restaurants nearby that are within a college student's budget such as Zorba's (really good gyros), Old World Pizza (they use whole basil leaves in their pizza), and Sakura Express."

Q "Hands-down **the most popular restaurant among students is Sakura Express.** The friendly owners serve sushi rolls and other Japanese dishes that are relatively cheap and fast."

Q "Thai Village serves up an **excellent Pad Thai.** It is BYOB and is a popular meeting place for birthday parties or large groups."

Q "For special occasions, **Princeton students often get their parents to take them to the Ferry House**, which serves traditional food made from local organic ingredients at prices above most student budgets."

Q "There are a bunch of restaurants within walking distance; the **food ranges from quick sandwiches to decent Chinese and Thai.** There are several pretty nice restaurants on Nassau Street and Palmer Square that are pretty expensive."

Q "**PJ's Pancake House is the best** breakfast you could ask for."

Q "Teresa's and JB Winberries are popular. If you have a car, there are other good ones within driving distance. **There are a lot of places in Princeton Market Fair** and Mercer Mall."

Q "The restaurants in Princeton are wonderful. **You have the best coffee house, Small World.** Of course you have fast food, delis, etc."

Q "Some favorites are PJ's Pancake House, JB Winberries, and Triumph Brewery, but I must warn you that **Princeton is a pretty expensive town.**"

The College Prowler Take On...
Off-Campus Dining

Recently, Princeton restaurants have started to diversify. Now it is possible to sample a wide variety of ethnic cuisines, whereas four years ago, selection was limited. New Jersey's top rated sushi restaurant, Ajihei, is a two-minute walk from campus. Students have made a cult of Witherspoon Street's Sakura Express, sending postcards from around the world to the two sushi chefs. Aside from the inexpensive Burger King on Nassau Street, students also favor the takeout Greek deli Olives and the takeout Greek restaurant Zorba's. Several mid-range options, such as the popular Italian Teresa's provide options for nicer nights out. High-end restaurants, including the Ferry House and Mediterra, are popular amongst wealthy "townies" and parents in for the weekend.

For a town its size, Princeton offers dozens of restaurant options. Some restaurants in town are certainly too expensive for a student's budget, but those restaurants are generally saved for special occasions, such as Parent's Weekend. If there is a cuisine that is not represented by Princeton's restaurants, it is easy enough to get on a train and find something in New York.

B+

The College Prowler™ Grade on
Off-Campus Dining: B+

"A high off campus dining grade implies that off campus restaurants are affordable, accessible, and worth visiting. Other factors include the variety of cuisine and the availability of alternative options (vegetarian, vegan, kosher, etc.)"

On-Campus Housing

The Lowdown On...
On-Campus Housing

Undergraduates in Dormitories:
97%

Best Dorms:
Patton Hall
Little Hall
Witherspoon Hall
Blair Hall
1915 Hall
1903 Hall

Worst Dorms:
1940 Hall
1941 Hall
Forbes Annex
Cuyler Hall
Brown Hall
Wilcox Hall

Princeton Owned Housing Units:
Singles: 53%
Doubles: 23%
Triples/Suites: 22%
Apartments: 2%

Room Types:

Housing runs the gamut at Princeton, and there is no general formula. Many of Princeton's dorms were built before modern amenities were standard in homes, so older buildings have been added to in order to accommodate changing times. The size of a Princeton room is not standard as well. Some buildings will include a range of rooms from singles to 11-person suites. (The Housing Department is also notorious for placing extra students in a room if there is a housing crunch, so, for instance, rooms that were once large singles are now tiny doubles.) The furniture in each of the dorms is as varied as the dorms themselves. The newer dorms all have new furniture that is pretty standard, and students are not permitted to remove it from their rooms. The older dorms have both twin and extra-long twin beds and a mish-mash of furniture. Some rooms do not have closets or any other form of pre-installed storage. Incoming freshmen should buy extra long sheets on the theory that they will get a long bed at least once at Princeton, and it is impossible to fit a regular twin fitted sheet on an extra-long bed.

The simplest way to approach housing at Princeton is by designation. Freshmen and sophomores are split into five residential colleges: Butler, Forbes, Mathey, Rockefeller ("Rocky"), and Wilson. Construction is underway for a sixth college, Whitman, but it will not be ready for several years. Each college has its own dining hall and residential and academic staffs. Generally, the residential staff who assigns rooms tries to keep residential college dorms balanced by gender and by class year. Each dorm section has a residential advisor (RA) and a minority affairs advisor (MAA) or, in Wilson College, a residential community advisor (RCA) and a residential community program advisor (RCPA). Juniors are seniors are spread across campus in the bevy of upperclass dorms, and there are no limits to the number of members of each gender and class who draw into specific rooms and dorms, which can create for crowded bathroom situations, as most upperclass bathrooms are shared by floor.

Dormitories:

2 Dickinson Street

Designation: Upperclass
Floors: 3 + Lower Level
Bathrooms: Shared by Floor
Co-Ed: Yes
Room Types: Single, Double
Special Features: Vegetarian co-op in the building, study area, laundry

99 Alexander Street

Designation: Forbes College
Floors: 2 + Lower Level
Bathrooms: Shared by Floor
Co-Ed: No. Female only.
Room Types: Single, Double, Triple
Special Features: This "Pink House," is literally a pink house owned by the University to house girls in Forbes College. It features a living room, dining room, and two kitchens.

1901 Hall

Designation: Upperclass
Floors: 4
Bathrooms: Shared by Floor
Co-Ed: Yes
Room Types: Single, Double, Triple, Quad, Suite

1903 Hall

Designation: Upperclass
Floors: 4 + Basement
Bathrooms: Shared by Floor
Co-Ed: Yes
Room Types: Single, Double, Triple, Quad
Special Features: Kitchen, Laundry

1915 Hall

Designation: Butler College
Floors: 2 + Basement
Bathrooms: Basement
Co-Ed: No. One side male, One side female.
Room Types: Triples (Male), Singles and Doubles (Female)
Special Features: Laundry

1922 Hall

Designation: Butler College
Floors: 2 + Basement
Bathrooms: Shared by Floor
Co-Ed: Yes
Room Types: Single, Double, Suite
Special Features: Music Practice Room

1927-Clapp Hall

Designation: Wilson College

Floors: 3 + Basement

Bathrooms: In-Room, Shared by Floor

Co-Ed: Yes

Room Types: Double, Quad, Suite

Special Features: Laundry Room, Game Room

1937 Hall

Designation: Wilson College

Floors: 3 + Ground Floor

Bathrooms: Shared by Floor, In-Room

Co-Ed: Yes

Room Types: Single, Double, Suite

1938 Hall

Designation: Wilson College

Floors: 3 + Basement

Bathrooms: Shared by Floor, In-Suite

Co-Ed: Yes

Room Types: Single, Double, Suite

1939 Hall

Designation: Wilson College

Floors: 4 + Basement

Bathrooms: Shared by Floor, In-Suite

Co-Ed: Yes

Room Types: Single, Double, Suite

1940 Hall

Designation: Butler College

Floors: 3

Bathrooms: Shared by Floor

Co-Ed: Yes

Room Types: Single, Double, Suite

1941 Hall

Designation: Butler College

Floors: 3 + Basement

Bathrooms: Shared by Floor

Co-Ed: Yes

Room Types: Single, Double, Suite

1942 Hall

Designation: Butler College

Floors: 3 + Basement

Bathrooms: Shared by Floor

Co-Ed: Yes

Room Types: Single, Double, Suite

Special Features: Computer Cluster

Blair Hall

Designation: Rocky College, Mathey College

Floors: 4 + Basement

Bathrooms: Shared by Floor

Co-Ed: Yes

Room Types: Single, Double, Triple, Quad

Special Features: Lounge, Study Rooms, Seminar Room, Blair Arch, Home of the famous Princeton a cappella arch sings

Brown Hall

Designation: Upperclass

Floors: 4 + Basement

Bathrooms: Shared by Floor

Co-Ed: Yes

Room Types: Single, Double, Triple, Quad

Special Features: Kitchen

Campbell Hall

Designation: Mathey College

Floors: 3 + Basement

Bathrooms: Basement

Co-Ed: No. Female Only.

Room Types: Single, Double, Triple, Quad

Special Features: Fitness Room

Cuyler Hall

Designation: Upperclass

Floors: 3 + Basement

Bathrooms: Basement

Co-Ed: Yes

Room Types: Single, Double, Triple, Quad, Suite

Special Features: Kitchen

Dod Hall

Designation: Upperclass

Floors: 5 + Basement

Bathrooms: Shared by Floor

Co-Ed: Yes

Room Types: Singles, Triples

Special Features: Kitchen, Laundry, Study Rooms

Dodge-Osborn Hall

Designation: Wilson College

Floors: 3 + Basement + Ground Floor

Bathrooms: Shared by Floor, In-Suite

Co-Ed: Yes

Room Types: Single, Double, Suite

Special Features: Kitchen

Edwards Hall

Designation: Upperclass

Floors: 5 + Basement

Bathrooms: Shared by Floor

Co-Ed: Yes

Room Types: Single, Double

Special Features: Kitchen, Computer Cluster

Feinberg Hall

Designation: Wilson College

Floors: 4 + Ground Floor

Bathrooms: Shared by Floor, In-Room

Co-Ed: Yes

Room Types: Single, Double, Triple, Suite

Special Features: Laundry Room

Forbes Annex

Designation: Forbes College

Floors: 4 + Basement

Bathrooms: Shared by Floor

Co-Ed: Yes

Room Types: Single, Double

Special Features: Kitchen, Lounge, Laundry

Forbes Main Inn

Designation: Forbes College

Floors: 4 + Basement

Bathrooms: In-Room

Co-Ed: Yes

Room Types: Single, Double, Triple

Special Features: Kitchen, Computer Cluster, Music Room, Laundry, Theater, TV Room, Library

Foulke Hall

Designation: Upperclass

Floors: 4 + Basement

Bathrooms: Shared by Floor

Co-Ed: Yes

Room Types: Single, Double, Triple, Quad

Gauss Hall

Designation: Wilson College

Floors: 2 + Basement

Bathrooms: Shared by Floor

Co-Ed: Yes

Room Types: Single, Double, Suite

Special Features: Computer Cluster

Hamilton Hall

Designation: Mathey College

Floors: 2 + Ground Floor

Bathrooms: Basement

Co-Ed: Yes

Room Types: Single, Double, Triple, Quad

Special Features: College Office, Conference Room

Henry Hall

Designation: Upperclass

Floors: 5 + Ground Floor

Bathrooms: Shared by Floor

Co-Ed: Yes

Room Types: Single, Double, Triple, Quad, Suite

Special Features: Kitchen, Laundry

Holder Hall

Designation: Rocky College

Floors: 3 + Basement

Bathrooms: Basement, Shared by Floor

Co-Ed: Yes

Room Types: Single, Double, Triple, Quad, Suite

Special Features: Laundry, Lounge, Library, Conference Room

Joline Hall

Designation: Mathey College

Floors: 3 + Basement

Bathrooms: Basement

Co-Ed: No. Male Only.

Room Types: Single, Double, Triple, Quad

Special Features: Lounge, Laundry

Laughlin Hall

Designation: Upperclass

Floors: 3 + Ground Floor

Bathrooms: Shared by Entryway

Co-Ed: Yes

Room Types: Single, Double, Triple, Quad

Special Features: Kitchen

Little Hall

Designation: Upperclass

Floors: 4 + Basement + Ground Floor

Bathrooms: Shared by Floor

Co-Ed: Yes

Room Types: Single, Double, Triple, Quad

Special Features: Lounge, Laundry Room, Laundry

Lourie-Love Hall

Designation: Butler College

Floors: 4 + Basement

Bathrooms: Shared by Floor

Co-Ed: Yes

Room Types: Single, Double, Suite

Special Features: Lounge, Laundry Room

Patton-Wright Hall

Designation: Upperclass

Floors: 5 + Basement

Bathrooms: Shared by Floor

Co-Ed: Yes

Room Types: Single, Double, Triple, Quad, Suite

Special Features: Laundry

Pyne Hall

Designation: Upperclass

Floors: 4 + Basement

Bathrooms: Shared by Floor

Co-Ed: Yes

Room Types: Single, Double, Triple, Quad

Special Features: Kitchen

Scully Hall

Designation: Upperclass

Floors: 4

Bathrooms: Shared by Floor, In-Room

Co-Ed: Yes

Room Types: Single, Double, Quad

Special Features: Kitchen, Laundry Rooms, Air Conditioning

Spelman Hall

Designation: Upperclass

Floors: 4 + Basement

Bathrooms: In-Room

Co-Ed: Yes

Room Types: Suites with Kitchens, Dining Area, and Bathroom

Special Features: Married Housing, Laundry Room, Vending Machines

Walker Hall

Designation: Upperclass, Butler College, Wilson College

Floors: 3 + Basement + Ground Floor

Bathrooms: Shared by Floor

Co-Ed: Yes

Room Types: Single, Double, Quad

Wilcox Hall

Designation: Wilson College

Floors: Third Floor of Main Wilson College Building

Bathrooms: Shared by Floor

Co-Ed: Yes

Room Types: Single, Double

Special Features: Dining Hall

Witherspoon Hall

Designation: Rocky College

Floors: 5 + Basement

Bathrooms: Shared by Floor

Co-Ed: Yes

Room Types: Single, Double, Quad

Special Features: Laundry Room, Kitchen, Study Rooms, Lounge

Cleaning Service?

Yes, in public areas only.

You Get:

Bed, dresser, Internet access, desk, desk chair, telephone jack

Also Available:

Substance-free areas, smoke-free areas, special needs housing, independent housing

Did You Know?

Princeton's dormitories are currently undergoing **an extensive renovation program**. Each year, one large or two small dormitories close to undergo renovation, which includes replacement of the entire infrastructure of a dorm, including heating, plumbing, and electrical and data wiring.

The dorm where **John F. Kennedy** lived before transferring to Harvard is no longer standing.

In the mid-twentieth century, Princeton students were **responsible for bringing all of their own furniture**.

F. Scott Fitzgerald's *This Side of Paradise* depicts, in part, **residential life at Princeton** at the start of the twentieth century.

Students Speak Out On...
On-Campus Housing

> "Pack your shower shoes. The shower itself may not be too bad, but you may have several flights of stairs to walk down before reaching a bathroom."

Q "The residential colleges for underclassmen range in terms of rooms. **Some have bathrooms; some don't.** Some are new; some are old and crappy. Freshman year, I lived in a two-room triple that was about 280 square feet—not that big. Upperclassmen housing also ranges. If you get a good room draw time, you can draw into large singles or suites. 1903 Hall has nice singles. If you want newer rooms with air conditioning, Scully Hall is a good bet. In terms of central location, 1903 Hall, Brown Hall, and Cuyler Hall are all good places."

Q "They are all **rather nice and have lots of gothic-type architecture.** Appearance-wise, some of newer buildings are not as impressive as others, but all have similar living conditions. I enjoy it very much. The social scene is a little monotonous, and some of the fellow students are a little pretentious, but on the whole, it's a great place to have a college experience."

Q "Freshman year, there isn't a choice, but **you should be okay.** Sophomore year you live in the same general area but can pick your room. By junior year, you know where the best place to live will be—it varies with construction."

Q "Some dorms are gothic and old and pretty. Others are modern and ugly. All told, **they're in good shape.**"

Q "Generally, **freshmen rooms are not that bad.** You may have to share a bedroom and closet with two other people, but you usually have a common room as buffer."

Q "If you have allergies, try to **draw into Scully, because it is the only air-conditioned dorm on campus.** If you have serious medical problems, try drawing in Special Needs housing. The Housing Office will pick your room for you, but they will at least take your needs into account."

Q "If you have serious issues with smoking or drinking, definitely draw **smoke free or substance free housing.** The people who draw these rooms generally keep to themselves, but your room won't smell like an ashtray, or worse, when you move in."

Q "Dorms are fine…. **Everyone lives on campus**, so everyone is in the same boat; it's just fun to live with everyone. Mathey, Rocky, and Wilson are great residential colleges. Butler is yucky, although people really like the people that live down there. You'll love wherever you live. We still argue over who had the best residential college experience."

Q "You don't get much choice freshman year; **it's random,** but you can choose how many roommates you want. Sophomore year, you choose within the same college by lottery. Junior year, you can move into the nicer, upperclassmen dorms. Forbes College is perhaps the nicest, but it's farther from everything. Rocky and Mathey are nice and have the old Gregorian style. Butler and Wilson are more 'modern' and ugly, in my opinion."

Q "Room draw **can either be your best friend or your worst enemy.** Just hope for a good draw time, or you may be living in a glorified broom closet. If you get one of the top draw times, you can usually get a huge room in the middle of campus."

Q "Princeton's janitorial staff works really hard at keeping the dorms as nice and clean as possible. Unfortunately, they often go unrecognized, so **it is important to develop a good relationship with your janitor as early as possible.** Freshman year, we bought our janitor Knicks tickets, and she would always give us a heads up about fire inspections. Senior year, however, we threw a couple of parties towards the end of the year and had our trash cans confiscated."

Q "It is **pretty difficult to find the 'ideal' dorm at Princeton.** Not all dorms have laundry rooms. Some have been renovated recently, most have not. Dod Hall, for example, was redone a couple of years ago and has new laundry and kitchen facilities, but the bedrooms are half the size of most of the upperclass bedrooms on campus."

Q "The dorms are all really nice. **All the dorms are close to the academic buildings**, but Forbes dorm is pretty far if you want to get to the E-Quad."

Q "Students select rooms each spring in a process called room draw. Room draw is one of those processes in which the higher ups are happy and everyone else is miserable. Junior year, I lived in the largest double on campus, 450-square feet with three closets. Senior year, I found myself at the bottom of draw and opted to live with friends in a hallway of small singles. **My room was 133-square feet and did not have a closet.**"

Q "The dorms are, overall, pretty nice. **They're mostly gothic**, however freshman and sophomore year, you could get stuck in Butler and Wilson, where the buildings are not as pretty. Usually, people live in suites, where there are a few bedrooms and a common room, but you can also get a single or a double if you want."

Q "**Dorms vary.** You don't get to choose your freshman-year room, so it wouldn't help to list good and bad dorms. Nothing is intolerable, though, and they're pretty clean. Some rooms are like gothic churches. Some are standard college rooms. Dorms are drawn on a lottery; you really do not have a choice. About the living situation on campus—you are required to live in a residential college for your freshman and sophomore years. There are five colleges on campus. Basically, the colleges are a group of dorms clustered together, and each college has its own dining hall. Your meal plan will allow you to eat at any of them."

Q "**Each college has its own ups and downs.** Wilson College, which is located in the center of campus, has some of the largest suites—like 12 people to a room—and tons of singles for sophomores, but the buildings are pretty ugly. You are randomly assigned to a college freshman year and can choose your room sophomore year. All of the colleges have links on the Princeton website, so you can check them out there. After sophomore year, there are tons of upperclassmen dorms to choose from. Butler College is bad; Blair Hall is really nice."

The College Prowler Take On...
On-Campus Housing

Generally, students are pleased with their housing experience, but they realize that is more of a reflection on the experience rather than the accommodations. While the "upper-campus" residential colleges, Rocky and Mathey, are attractive on the outside, students in the "lower-campus" residential colleges, Butler, Wilson, and Forbes, complain about "waffle ceilings" and far walks. As far as upperclass housing, the quality of your dorm depends on your draw time and personal preference. Whereas one student may like the air-conditioning of Scully, others would complain about its lack of proximity to the rest of the upperclass dorms and live in a smaller, un-air-conditioned room in Brown, Dod, or Edwards.

Princeton's housing options could be better...a lot better. Students view campus housing as a bonding experience, and only 3% opt out of it. With few affordable options within walking distance to campus, the University has little incentive to improve the conditions in the dorms, as it knows the students have few other options. In a recent move to improve living conditions on campus, however, the University has started to renovate one large dorm or two small dorms a year. This is a long-awaited improvement, considering that many students in some of the older Gothic dorms still have to walk down four flights of stairs to use a washroom. Generally, the best place to live on campus is the one that was most recently renovated, regardless of the size of the rooms.

The College Prowler™ Grade on
Campus Housing: C+

"A high Campus Housing grade indicates that dorms are clean, well-maintained and spacious. Other determining factors include variety of dorms, proximity to classes and social atmosphere."

Off-Campus Housing

The Lowdown On...
Off-Campus Housing

Undergrads in Off-Campus Housing:
3%

Best Time to Look for a Place:
Spring

Average Rent for a Studio Apartment:
$825/month

Average Rent for a One-Bedroom Apartment:
$1,100/month

Average Rent for a Two-Bedroom Apartment:
$1,570/month

Popular Areas:
Princeton
Princeton Junction

Students Speak Out On...
Off-Campus Housing

"There really isn't much off-campus housing; there aren't any nearby apartments or such. One of my friends lived 20 minutes off campus in another town, but not many people do that. On-campus housing is provided for all four years."

Q "Just about **everyone lives on campus.** Off-campus housing is very expensive due to the nature of the Princeton area, but on-campus housing is really good."

Q "It's not that it isn't convenient, it's just that **nobody really lives off campus.**"

Q "**Barely anyone** lives off campus."

Q "There's not much of it, but no worry ... **you're guaranteed on-campus housing for all four years.** There are some really sweet rooms on campus, and also some pretty small ones. Generally, it gets better as you get older. Your best chance of living off campus in a really nice room is to become an eating club officer and live there—you get awesome rooms."

Q "Off-campus housing is available, but **no one really chooses it** because on campus is generally really good."

Q "Students are guaranteed on-campus housing for four years, so **you don't have to worry about finding an apartment.**"

Q "Off-campus housing basically **does not exist.** Apartments off campus are very expensive, and there's so much going on that no one ever wants to leave anyway. I don't know anybody who doesn't live on campus."

Q "There's really no reason to live off campus. **It's expensive and really inconvenient.** Almost everyone, without exception, lives in on-campus housing all four years. Housing at Princeton is pretty good. You will live comfortably, but do not expect the Ritz Carlton. The new fitness center in the gym is incredible."

Q "Off-campus housing is **very expensive** and not convenient. Most students have no desire to leave on-campus housing."

Q "Everyone pretty much lives on campus. Not only is it the most convenient, but there is really **nowhere in the town of Princeton that would be convenient for students.** Princeton is a really expensive suburb; everyone lives on campus."

The College Prowler Take On...
Off-Campus Housing

Students cannot elect to live off campus until junior year, so most students grow accustomed to the daily housekeeping service in communal dorm areas, particularly bathrooms and hallways, during their freshman and sophomore years. Because Princeton is such an affluent town, particularly in the areas surrounding the campus, off-campus housing is not financially feasible to the majority of the undergraduate population.

To find an affordable option, students would need access to a car, which is still problematic, because parking near the academic buildings is close to non-existent. Once students find off-campus housing, they would have to install necessary features that are provided in on-campus housing, such as Ethernet, and then they would have to cope with the utter isolation of living off-campus. Basically, it is not worth it.

D-

The College Prowler™ Grade on

Off-Campus Housing: D-

A high grade in Off-Campus Housing indicates that apartments are of high quality, close to campus, affordable, and easy to secure.

Diversity

The Lowdown On...
Diversity

White:
66%

International:
7%

Asian or Pacific Islander:
12%

Out of State:
85%

African American:
8%

American Indian:
1%

Hispanic:
6%

Political Activity:

The majority of Princeton students do not engage in campus political activity on a regular basis, but there is an active debate group, the Whig-Cliostrophic Society. The College Republicans and College Democrats also draw an energetic membership. There has also been a recent influx of campus political publications, notably the Princeton Tory, a conservative thought magazine. With so many Princeton alumni going into politics and so many politicians sending their children to Princeton, election time is always interesting.

Gay Tolerance:

Generally, the Princeton community is accepting of gay students, as seen by the popularity of Pride Alliance events. However, there is the occasional incident, such as anti-gay graffiti, that reminds students of a very small un-accepting minority.

Most Popular Religions:

Princeton has several very visible campus religious groups, such as Agape, Athletes in Action, and the Center for Jewish Life. Princeton's Religious Life Office gives students many on-campus options and outlets for religious practice, including weekly meditation and prayer meetings in the University's recently renovated chapel.

Economic Status:

Even though Princeton has the reputation for being an elitist institution, Princeton attracts students of all economic backgrounds because of its recent no-loan program. Rather than forcing students to leave school debt-ridden, Princeton now awards financial aid grants.

Sampling of Minority Clubs

Campus groups, such as Princeton South Asian Theatrics and Naacho, have helped raise awareness of minorities on campus. The Black Student Union has a board in Frist that allows for better publicity of minority events on campus.

Students Speak Out On...
Diversity

"The campus is mostly white, but there is a decent percentage of minorities. I guess the diversity could be a little better, but they are working on it."

Q "It's **extremely diverse.** There are people here from all over—different states, different countries—they are just from all over the place. It's pretty cool. You get to see a lot of different cultures out there, and people are very proud of their ethnicities."

Q "It's somewhat diverse, **depending on your definition of diversity.** People come from everywhere, from all walks of life, from all countries, etc. It actually is hugely interesting. The campus is working to admit more minorities, but I felt like my experience was diverse... my best friends were from all over and of many ethnicities."

Q "It's pretty diverse. **I met a lot of people** during various social events and at parties."

Q "The students **represent most of the world,** and because of the scene, you pretty much will interact with everyone from all different backgrounds."

Q "Compared to my high school, **Princeton is not diverse at all**, but my high school was also ranked one of the most diverse schools in the state, so maybe I'm biased. What makes the Princeton experience so exceptional is not necessarily the racial diversity but the diversity of student experience. While some students come from very isolated parts of the United States, such as rural Kansas, others come from cosmopolitan international centers."

Q "It's **not as diverse as many places.** It's largely white, but there are definitely minorities."

Q "It is predominantly **white upper-class**, but I'm Hispanic, and I know lots of people who are also Hispanic, African American, and Asian. I don't really find it to be much of an issue, but I probably wouldn't say that it's really diverse."

Q "We definitely have a variety of people. I don't know how diverse it is compared to other campuses, but I know there are all kinds of student organizations for different nationalities, races, religions, etc. **Being a minority will not prohibit you from doing anything at Princeton,** and most students really do not consider it a significant factor on campus."

The College Prowler Take On...
Diversity

Depending upon students' personal experience, some students think that Princeton is very diverse, and others think that there are few minorities at all. While not all students believe that Princeton is diverse, it is impossible to deny the range of student groups available to promote diversity awareness.

Princeton is not as diverse as some other Ivy League schools, but the school's demographics are diverse considering the racial and economic of the surrounding town. Diversity at Princeton is starting to improve, because the University has recently instituted a no-loan financial aid program, which ensures that all financial aid will be given in the form of grants that do not need to be repaid. An increasing number of discussion forums have also helped raise awareness of campus diversity issues.

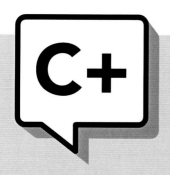

The College Prowler™ Grade on

Diversity: C+

A high grade in Diversity indicates that ethnic minorities and international students have a notable presence on campus, and that students of different economic backgrounds, religious beliefs, and sexual preferences are well-represented.

Guys & Girls

The Lowdown On...
Guys & Girls

Women Undergrads:	Men Undergrads:
48%	52%

Birth Control Available?

Yes. Sexuality Education Counseling and Health Office (S.E.C.H.), McCosh Health Center. Female students who have had an annual exam with their home doctor or have an exam with the S.E.C.H. Office can have their birth control prescriptions filled at health services for a discounted fee. S.E.C.H. offers all forms of birth control: birth control pills, patches, diaphragms, contraceptive gel, and Depo-Provera injections. S.E.C.H. also sells discounted condoms.

Most Prevalent STDs on Campus:

Genital warts (HPV), Herpes

Social Scene:

Like any university, Princeton students range from studious ones who rarely go out to those who can hardly be called students. For some students, Princeton provides a "work hard, party hard" environment, which is initially surprising because of the rigor of Princeton's academic program. Contrary to popular belief, not all Princeton students are nerds or trust fund kids, so most find their niche quickly. Unfortunately, the Greek scene, strong athletic teams, and eating clubs slightly fragment the student body, but they also help some students gain some sort of identity of campus.

Hookups or Relationships?

The Princeton hookup scene is relatively isolated to underclass girls and upperclass men. By junior and senior year, Princeton women generally date or get involved in serious relationships, while Princeton men play the field more. Because male Princeton freshmen are at the absolute bottom of any dating hierarchy, they tend to remain in relationships from high school rather than face rejection from the women on campus.

Best Place to Meet Guys/Girls:

The best place to meet other students initially is in residential colleges, whether it is in the dining hall or in one's RA group, which helps give freshmen social options on campus. Fraternity and sorority rush starts several weeks after the freshmen arrive on campus, and the Greek scene draws a small fraction of students into Greek life. For everyone else, social interaction can occur on a regular basis anywhere from "The Street" to campus religious gatherings. Princeton students are notorious for getting spring fever, or simply frolicking whenever the weather is warm. Mysteriously, the rate of random hookups seems to increase during warm weather periods, such as Freshman Week and in the spring. (This may also be a correlation between relatively slow work periods.)

Did You Know?

Top Three Places to Find Hotties:

1. The Eating Clubs
2. Frist Campus Center
3. Dining halls

Top Places to Hookup:

1. Eating clubs
2. Empty classrooms—Frist and the E-Quad
3. Dorm Singles
4. Firestone Library carrels
5. Athletic fields

Dress Code:

Generally, Princeton students represent a happy medium between preppy and fashionable. It is rare to see a student show up to class in sweatpants or anything resembling pajamas. Few students have what could be called an "urban, edgy" look. Guys usually wear polo shirts and khakis, and girls wear comfortable, stylish clothes. Recent uniforms have included Lilly Pulitzer attire, Longchamp bags, and Seven and Paper Denim jeans.

Students Speak Out On...
Guys & Girls

> "The guys are cool but a little pretentious, and the girls are very pretentious. The majority is ugly as sin—only a few good-looking ones exist, half of which have boyfriends. The idea of 'importing girls' is widely used."

Q "Freshman year, **my RA told me that nobody dates at Princeton**. Personally, I have not found that to be true, but I can see how someone would."

Q "A lot of people at Princeton are **pretty wealthy.** It is also mostly white. I guess from this, there can be a lot of stuck-up snobs, but most of the people I met were very cool and down-to-earth. The girls are okay, although they definitely don't compare to some other schools in terms of looks. The guys pretty much agree that there aren't a lot of hot chicks on campus."

Q "Not only are the girls cute, but they are also **smart, nice, non-scary, etc.** The only downside is that as Princeton tends to have people who are used to success, guys tend to fear the whole asking-out thing. We have a lot of serious couples and hookups but minimal dating."

Q "I found the majority of girls to be attractive. It seemed that there were an **abnormally large percentage of hot girls.** I didn't pay much attention to the guys."

Q "People here are pretty diverse and the gamut from **bookish nerds to party animals.**"

Q "There's probably a pretty big spectrum, but hot guys are definitely available. **I'm quite satisfied with the guys on campus.** As for the girls, well, I think we're really good-looking as well."

Q "The guys are 50/50. As for the girls, they are spilt, too. You have the **stuck-up rich snobs**, and then you have the everyday girl, who is friendly and loves to go out and make new friends. You have to remember, though, that there are three other major colleges within 30 minutes of you, so you can always meet people form other schools when you go out. You are not limited to just Princeton kids; you have Rutgers, College of New Jersey, and Rider, and within an hour, you have all the New York and Philly schools. People are never a problem and neither are hot guys."

Q "There are **very good looking people** at Princeton."

Q "You have a **nice selection of good-looking guys** and girls if you go to the right places. Generally, if you go to the eating clubs on a Thursday or Saturday night, you'll find the best-looking people on campus. However, don't expect to find too many in a 300-level math class. On the whole, I'd say the people on campus are better-looking than most colleges, and many outsiders have said the same."

Q "On the whole, there are attractive people here. After visiting, a friend of mine described Princeton as being **full of 'beautiful, disgruntled people.'** I don't know if I agree about disgruntled, though. Princeton people are fairly good-looking. A recent study has shown that about a third of Princeton alums marry other Princeton alums. Read into that however you like. They're not naturally gorgeous so much, but well kempt, if that makes sense. They take care of themselves and are attractive."

The College Prowler Take On...
Guys & Girls

With the pressures of getting into a top-tier school like Princeton, many of the matriculating students missed some of the more active social lives that their high school classmates had the opportunity to experience. Socializing freshman year is awkward at best. Freshman girls are pursued by the more experienced upperclassmen while freshman boys wait for their turns to come. After a freshman year of casual dating or hooking up, Princeton women plunge to the bottom of the dating totem pole by senior year when they see their male classmates attempt to chase the younger women on campus.

It is difficult to place a single stereotype on the Princeton man or Princeton women, as many of us would like to think that we are like alumni Dean Cain '88 and Brooke Shields '87, but the diversity of student character and experience makes it difficult to pigeonhole everyone. There are few amazingly attractive men or women on campus, but everyone knows about them, if not only because of the Nassau Weekly's annual top ten list. Princeton students generally try to take care of themselves, so while there is no danger of running into the next hottest supermodel, it is easy to surround yourself with attractive, witty, well-educated people.

The College Prowler™ Grade on
Guys: B

A high grade for Guys indicates that the male population on campus is attractive, smart, friendly, and engaging, and that the school has a decent ratio of guys to girls.

The College Prowler™ Grade on
Girls: B

A high grade for Girls not only implies that the women on campus are attractive, smart, friendly, and engaging, but also that there is a fair ratio of girls to guys.

Athletics

The Lowdown On...
Athletics

Athletic Division:
NCAA Division I

Conference:
Ivy League

School Mascot:
Tiger

Fields:
Clarke Field
Lourie-Love Field
Princeton Battlefield

→

Intercollegiate Varsity Sports

Men's Teams:

Football

Football-Sprint

Basketball

Baseball

Crew-Heavyweight

Crew-Lightweight

Cross Country

Fencing

Golf

Hockey

Lacrosse

Soccer

Squash

Swimming & Diving

Tennis

Track And Field, Indoor

Track And Field, Outdoor

Volleyball

Water Polo

Wrestling

Women's Teams:

Basketball

Crew-Open

Crew-Lightweight

Cross Country

Fencing

Field Hockey

Golf

(Women's Teams, continued)

Hockey

Lacrosse

Soccer

Softball

Squash

Swimming & Diving

Tennis

Track And Field, Indoor

Track And Field, Outdoor

Volleyball

Water Polo

Club Sports:

Aikido

Badminton

Ballroom Dance

Baseball

Basketball—Men's

Basketball—Women's

Cricket

Cycling

Equestrian

Field Hockey

Figure Skating

Ice Hockey—Men's

Ice Hockey—Women's

Karate

Kendo

Lacrosse—Men's

Lacrosse—Women's

(Club Sports, continued)	Intramurals:
Rifle	Badminton
Rugby—Men's	Basketball
Rugby—Women's	Bowling
Running	Broomball
Sailing	Floor Hockey
Shotokan Karate	Fooseball
Ski & Snowboard	Golf
Soccer—Men's	Ice Hockey
Soccer—Women's	Inner-tube Water Polo
Softball	Soccer
Table Tennis	Softball
Taekwondo	Tennis
Tennis	
Ultimate Frisbee—Men's	
Ultimate Frisbee—Women's	
Volleyball—Men's	
Volleyball—Women's	

Getting Tickets:

Students do not need to pay for many sporting events, and tickets are not difficult to obtain. Occasionally, it is necessary to get tickets ahead of time, but that is usually for major events, such as a Princeton-Penn home basketball game.

Most Popular Sports:

On the varsity level, the most visible teams are the football, basketball, baseball, ice hockey, and lacrosse teams. Football games draw in droves of alumni, especially for games against Big Three rivals Harvard and Yale. A strong rivalry with Penn in basketball gives Princeton students something to cheer about during the icy winters. Both lacrosse teams—men's and women's—have pulled in multiple national titles in recent history and are a great source of school spirit.

Overlooked Teams:

The squash program is probably one of the most successful but underappreciated athletic programs on campus. Each year, the team places well in national tournaments but gets little exposure on campus, perhaps because few students even know what squash is by the time they get to campus freshman year. On the club level, both rugby teams have had great runs in national tournaments recently, but, because of its status as a club sport, rugby does not get the same sort of exposure as the football or lacrosse teams.

Best Place to Take a Walk:

Towpath around Lake Carnegie, Princeton Battlefield

Gyms/Facilities:

Baker Rink

Baker Rink is one of the older athletic facilities on campus, but constant attention from alumni donors has ensured that it remains in good condition. Recently, a giant, orange 'P' was added to the center of the ice, and a new refrigeration system as well as improved tempered glass and fiberglass boards have been added to improve the appearance of the facility. Students are able to use the rink occasionally for free skating when it is not in use by either of the ice hockey teams, the figure skating team, or any intramural teams.

Class of 1952 Stadium

The Class of 1952 Field, the home field for the nationally ranked field hockey and men's and women's lacrosse teams, was converted into Princeton's first artificial turf stadium in 1995. Lights on the field make night games and practices possible, which is particularly useful for club teams.

DeNunzio Pool

DeNunzio Pool was constructed in 1990 with modern design and technology, making it among the fastest pools in the nation. The building includes bleachers to accommodate 1,700 spectators, men's and women's locker rooms, an exercise room, offices and a conference room. Because it houses the University's Diving Team, DeNunzio also includes complete diving facilities. A tunnel system connects the pool building to adjacent Jadwin Gym and Caldwell Fieldhouse.

Dillon Gymnasium

Dillon Gymnasium, the former home of the basketball team, is the intramural sports and physical education headquarters with four basketball courts, 19 squash courts, an extensive fitness center and a pool. It also serves as the home arena for the men's and women's volleyball teams and the wrestling team and can accommodate nearly 1,500 spectators.

Jadwin Gymnasium

Jadwin Gymnasium is a multipurpose athletic facility that has a combined floor space of approximately 250,000 square feet, more total area than eight football fields. Jadwin includes facilities for the basketball, track and field, fencing, squash, tennis, wrestling, and baseball teams, including an eight-laps-per-mile track, one of the largest fencing rooms in the world, and 10 international-sized squash courts with spectator galleries to name a few. Jadwin has hosted professional exhibitions and national tournaments, and it is used as an indoor practice facility for many outdoor sports on days of bad weather. The main floor is surrounded by permanent seating for 6,854 spectators.

Lenz Tennis Center

Consisting of eight lighted courts and seating for 700 spectators, the Lenz Tennis Center has served as host for numerous collegiate championship events. As the main hub of Princeton's 35 courts, the center also boasts a clubhouse with office facilities.

Princeton Stadium

Princeton Stadium opened several years ago to replace the rapidly deteriorating Palmer Stadium, the second oldest football stadium in the country, which had to be demolished, because it was being reinforced by orange and black netting. This $45 million facility has a seating capacity of 27,800, with room for more than 30,000 in the building. Aside from hosting football games, Princeton Stadium is also used as a meeting and banquet place for many University constituents.

Shea Rowing Center

With one of the best crew programs with more than 200 athletes on the various teams in the country, Princeton's boathouse brags a recent renovation and state-of-the-art equipment. The new Shea Rowing Center includes modern facilities and equipment, such as a new rowing tank, larger locker and shower rooms, better heat and ventilation systems and improved handicap access, as well as offices and weight training areas. Additional launches, dockage and boat racks have been installed also.

Springdale Golf Club

The course is 6,380 yards from the championship (blue) tees and 6,017 yards from the men's (white) tees, with par at 71 for each. From the women's (red) tees the course is 5,599 yards and is a par 72. The entire driving range was upgraded in 1997. These renovations have improved the teams' practice capabilities.

Weaver Track, Field Stadium & Frelinghuysen Field

Princeton's new track and field stadium is part of the complex that replaced Palmer Stadium. Weaver Track, Field Stadium & Frelinghuysen Field brags additional running lanes, wider lanes, and a greater radius on the turns than were possible on the Palmer track. The stadium's track is made of durable brick red full-depth polyurethane, the safest, fastest and most comfortable surface available.

Students Speak Out On...
Athletics

{ **"Varsity sports are very big. Sports on campus are huge; it seems that nearly half or more of the student body participates in some athletics— varsity or IM."**

Q "Varsity sports are pretty big. Our football team isn't that good, so **basketball gets a lot of fans**, so does lacrosse. A very high percentage of the student body plays varsity sports. Everyone else plays club sports or intramurals (IM). Intramurals are pretty big and cover sports from hockey to flag football to basketball, etc. I played in a lot of IMs, and they were always competitive and a lot of fun."

Q "**A huge number of students participate**. Sports are pretty big simply because people always enjoy going and cheering on their friends."

Q "I love going to basketball games, **sometimes they can be very exciting**, especially if we are having a good season."

Q "There are lots of opportunities. **Varsity sports are pretty big and fairly good.** Field hockey, lacrosse, swimming, some individual track events, basketball, squash—all are competitive on the national level and some have several national titles. Football has been less consistent; although they won the Ivy League champs my first year. There are also club sports, which are sort of like varsity but officially a step below."

Q "There are a lot of sports and **always an IM team you can join.** It really just depends on who you hang out with and how much sports are a part of your life."

Q "IM sports are huge and so much fun! We have everything from broomball **(It's the best sport ever—hockey using brooms instead of pucks),** soccer, basketball, to inner tube water polo. They were a huge part of my Princeton experience. Not only did I have an awesome time and get great exercise, but I also met a lot of my close friends through them."

Q "I have been to all the pool events and a couple football and basketball games, and they seem to be pretty good, especially the water polo games. **There are really hot guys in Speedos; it is great!**"

Q "Princeton was ranked as one of the top ten jock schools in the country, except **here the jocks are smart.** IM sports are a lot of fun and quite popular."

Q "We have **a ton of varsity athletes**; it blows me away. IM sports are fairly big as well. Not too many students attend football games, but a heck of a lot attend men's basketball games. Our basketball team is always first or second in the Ivy League. Our lacrosse team has won the National Championship in recent years. Varsity sports are very big, and a lot of people play them."

The College Prowler Take On...
Athletics

Athletics—varsity, club, and intramural—play an important role on campus. At some point in their Princeton career, most students will have some exposure to campus athletics, whether it is attending a game of the title-winning men's lacrosse team at Class of 1952 Stadium or participating in a yoga class at Dillon Gym. For students who are not up to varsity level, there are plenty of opportunities to participate on a team whether it is on one of the spirited IM teams or one of the University's thirty-four club teams. Scenic features such as the wooded towpath and Lake Carnegie also encourage students to take a break from their work and go jogging along one of the University's trails.

As a small, Ivy League school, Princeton's athletic prowess is almost surprising. Unable to offer athletic scholarships or any other perquisites, the University draws athletes who come to Princeton not only because of some of the award-winning athletic teams but also because of the top-notch academics. The Ivy League provides a fantastic rivalry and gives Princeton students another venue for bragging about their abilities on and off the field, with or without the assistance of their repeated top rating, a rank most Princeton student will not let you forget.

A

The College Prowler™ Grade on
Athletics: A

A high grade in athletics indicates that students have school spirit, that sports programs are respected, that games are well-attended, and that intramurals are a prominent part of student life.

Nightlife

The Lowdown On...
Nightlife

Student Favorites:

Triumph Brewing Company

The Annex

T.I.

Colonial

Cottage

Cap and Gown

Tower

Useful Resources for Nightlife:

Word-of-mouth

Bars Close At:

12 a.m.-2 a.m.

Primary Areas With Nightlife:

"The Street"

Cheapest Place to Get a Drink:

"The Street"

→

Club Crawler:

One of the questions most frequently posed to Princeton students is: "What is an eating club?" Contrary to popular belief, an eating club is not Princeton's answer to student country clubs. Today, Princeton's eating clubs are a collection of eleven clubhouses lining Prospect Street that provide upperclassmen with a place to eat and socialize, but in the nineteenth century, eating clubs sprouted up along Prospect to provide upperclassmen with eating options other than the then-atrocious University dining facilities.

In addition to providing eating options, eating clubs also provide the largest social scene for Princeton students. Each Thursday and Saturday night, the "Street" opens up for students to kick back because of the relative dearth of social options available to Princeton students. Some clubs require only University ID to gain entrance while others ask for a special pass, which can be obtained by members. Recently, clubs under the scrutiny of the town have started to crack down on under-age drinking, making room parties a commonality for those under 21. For those who choose to attend parties on Prospect Street, the average out night begins at about midnight and will last until two or three. Some students complain about the lack of variety at the clubs, citing the ubiquitous DJ Bob, an area Top 40 DJ whose company works at a number of clubs in any given night, as a major annoyance. Despite this seeming lack of variety, the eating clubs draw exciting acts, such as a Led Zeppelin cover band and Maroon 5. The eating clubs also host formals including Casino Night, Winter Formals, and spring Houseparties, a three-day event consisting of a formal, semi-formal, and lawn parties.

Campus Club (1900)

http://campusclub.princeton.edu/

5 Prospect Ave., Princeton

(609) 258-0865

Type: Bicker, starting 2003-2004 academic year

After suffering from a low membership for several years, Campus Club now enjoys a healthy membership. The club has announced that it will try out a bicker process, because Princeton students simply like the idea of being selected.

Cap & Gown Club (1890)

http://www.princeton.edu/~capgown/

61 Prospect Ave., Princeton

(609) 921-9795

Type: Bicker

Cap & Gown Club, or Cap as most students call it, is generally the club where athletes, especially the track and field, softball, football, and field hockey teams, join, but it is starting to diversify to include more campus groups. Cap easily has the best salad bar on the Street. Noted alumni include Dean Cain '88 and Brooke Shields '87.

Charter Club (1901)

http://www.princeton.edu/~charter/

79 Prospect Ave., Princeton

(609) 924-2433

Type: Sign In

Charter used to be home to the majority of the University's engineers because of its proximity to the E-Quad, but its weekly pub nights and quality food have enabled the membership to expand. Charter members favor live bands to weekly DJs, and recent acts have included American Hi-Fi.

Cloister Inn (1912)

http://www.princeton.edu/~cloister/

65 Prospect Ave., Princeton

(609) 258-1380

Type: Sign In

Also known as the "boaters and floaters" club, Cloister's hot tub and healthy cuisine draws students primarily from the crew and swim teams. Popular events include "Boaters vs. Floaters" races and competitions. Aside from the notorious Cloister hot tub, the outgoing officers brought in a mechanical bull to celebrate sign ins week.

Colonial Club (1891)

http://www.colonialclub.com/

40 Prospect Ave., Princeton

(609) 924-0255

Type: Sign In

After almost folding in 2000, Colonial Club was taken over by members of the Class of 2002 and has enjoyed a soaring membership in the past few years. Bragging weekly pub nights with homemade pizza and quesadillas, Colonial provides a combination of members-only events, such as an annual wine tasting, as well as open events, including a bevy of opportunities to see DJ Bob.

Cottage Club (1886)

http://www.princeton.edu/~cotclub/

51 Prospect Ave., Princeton

(609) 921-6137

Type: Bicker

Modelled as a combination of a country cottage and an urban clubhouse, Cottage has tried in recent years to receive historic site status because of its role in the literature of former member F. Scott Fitzgerald '17, who wrote sections of *This Side of Paradise* in Cottage's library, as well its famous alumni, including former Senator Bill Bradley '65. Cottage's membership is primarily composed of student athletes as members of the Greek community.

Ivy Club (1879)

http://www.ivyclub.princeton.edu/

43 Prospect Ave., Princeton

(609) 924-2236

Type: Bicker

Ivy has always had the reputation for being the stomping grounds of Princeton's social aristocracy. While it is the only eating club whose members are served dinner on a nightly basis, using tablecloths nonetheless, its events are generally open to all students. Popular events include the annual T.I.-Ivy Olympics.

Quadrangle Club (1901)

http://quad.princeton.edu/

33 Prospect Ave., Princeton

(609) 258-0375

Type: Sign In

After several years of low turn out at sign ins, Quadrangle Club, or Quad, has started to turn around and is full again. Constantly seeking alternatives to DJ Bob, Quad tends to favor non-Bob DJs and live bands, including Lifehouse, who performed at Quad's 2003 spring lawn parties.

Terrace Club (1904)

http://www.princeton.edu/~terrace/

62 Washington Rd., Princeton

(609) 258-1380

Type: Sign In

Terrace provides an alternative environment to the other eating clubs. Not only is it the only club not located along Prospect, but it is the only club that permits cigarette smoking in the dining room. The tap room is painted black, and members tend to be a bit more artsy than the average Princeton student.

Tiger Inn (1890)

http://www.princeton.edu/~tigerinn/

48 Prospect Ave., Princeton

(609) 924–0255

Type: Bicker

Tiger Inn, or T.I., is the closest thing Princeton has to Animal House. Drawing from some of the more notoriously rowdy athletic teams, such as the men's lacrosse and wrestling teams, and Greek organizations, T.I. is the best place for late night partying. Many legends surround the T.I. cuisine, usually noting how members chose to eat hot dogs for a month rather than to go without Beast for the last month of school.

Tower Club (1902)

http://www.princeton.edu/~tower/

13 Prospect Ave., Princeton

(609) 924-0473

Type: Bicker

Tower is home to the majority of the campus politicians and thespians as well as some of the best desserts on the Street. The deck in the backyard allows Tower to throw parties almost every night during Freshman Week before most clubs are open. Members can elect to pay dues based on how much alcohol they consume. Those who claim to be "heavy drinkers" often can be found playing on one of the several Beirut tables in the taproom.

Bar Prowler:

For those over 21, there are three popular bars in town—The Annex, Triumph Brewery, and the Ivy Inn. The Annex is by far the most inexpensive and has the most personable staff. Triumph, a microbrewery, is popular among young area professionals and often hosts area bands during the weekend. It's great for cocktails. The Ivy Inn is the closest thing Princeton has to a dive bar and is popular for its weekly karaoke nights.

The Annex

128 1/2 Nassau St., Princeton

(609) 921-7555

Because of its proximity to Firestone Library, the Annex is popular with both students and faculty. The food and drinks are affordable, and the happy hour specials are difficult to pass. The Annex also hosts pub nights for the senior class each year.

Ivy Inn

248 Nassau St., Princeton

(609) 921-8555

The Ivy Inn, not to be confused with the Ivy Club, is conveniently adjacent to Hoagie Haven. Featuring nightly specials, the Ivy Inn does not even pretend to have any class, and it is a good place to go as an alternative to the Street.

JB Winberie Restaurant and Bar

1 Palmer Square East, # 1, Princeton

(609) 921-0700

Winberie's is popular with local 30-somethings at happy hour, but the bar is not a regular hang out for University undergrads. The bar is only a small component of Winberie's, which means that it gets crowded easily.

Triumph Brewing Company

138 Nassau St., Princeton

(609) 924-7855

While the beer and cocktails may be more expensive than what other bars in town have to offer, the atmosphere at Triumph is worth the cost. Whereas Winberie's is popular for young professionals in their 30s, local 20-somethings flock to Triumph. The beer is made on-site, and the food is fantastic.

Yankee Doodle Tap Room

10 Palmer Square East, Princeton

(609) 921-7500

Most students will not go to the Yankee Doodle Tap Room during their undergraduate career, as it is mostly Nassau Inn patrons who go there. The cocktails are relatively expensive for a student budget, and it has a definite feel of a hotel bar.

What to Do if You're Not 21:

Even if you are under 21, you can generally gain admission to Princeton's eating clubs, but the clubs are becoming increasingly diligent about checking I.D.s before serving alcohol.

Favorite Drinking Games:

Beer Pong

Beirut

Flip Cup

Quarters

Organization Parties:

Most student groups and athletic teams have parties during the academic year. These parties are primarily closed and used to recruit more members or bond with the existing ones. A Chinese restaurant called Good Friends in the adjacent Princeton Junction is a popular venue for such parties, as the alternative venues are rented eating clubs and campus suites.

Frats:

See the Greek Section!

Students Speak Out On...
Nightlife

"**The bars are okay; they're not really a big scene. The majority of the social scene is on campus. Most of the off-campus bar and club scene occurs in New York City, since it's only a $14 round trip train ride away.**"

Q "Because Princeton is a small town, **there aren't many bars and clubs off campus.** If you want to go clubbing, you probably have to go to New York; it's about an hour away by train. Ivy is a bar that's close to campus. Seniors will go there occasionally, but most of the social life revolves around 'The Street.' On weekends, eating clubs will have DJs, bands, parties, and free beer, so this is where people party. Clubs are usually open to everyone, although some clubs may have passes for special nights."

Q "**We don't really have clubs and bars off-campus.** The major social scene at Princeton evolves around the eating clubs which are on Prospect Street and basically on campus. There are 11 clubs, and every Thursday and Saturday (and some Fridays) they each have bands, DJs, or something going on. It's all free, all so much fun, and all very campus-orientated. I loved it because you always know that you will run into someone that you know, but at the same time, there are also tons and tons of people who you have never met."

Q "There are a **few places to drink off campus**, but most of the partying goes on in the eating clubs, which sort of like coed fraternities for upperclassmen. These cover a whole range of social interests, from the jock club (Cap and Gown) to the drinking club (Tiger Inn) to the mellow club (Campus) to the alternative club (Terrace), etc. If you really want to do the off-campus bar/club scene, you can drive a bit to get to nearby places down Route 1 or in Hope Town."

Q "I guess Triumph and the Annex would be the bars that people would go to although **most people stick to the social scene on campus**—the eating clubs."

Q "There are some nice sports in Princeton, but remember that New York is only an hour and a half away from Princeton. Philly is an hour away, and Trenton is only 30 minutes away. In Princeton, itself, you have the Ivy—they have bands play and make their own beer. New Hope has good clubs and bars. New Brunswick is where Rutgers University is; there is a whole bunch of college stuff to do around there, too. **Princeton is like a central location for almost every party and college spot in New Jersey**, because it is right in the middle of things."

Q "There are **a couple bars in town which aren't bad.** That said, most of the social scene takes place at the eating clubs, where most upperclassmen eat their meals. They throw parties and dances and are 'on tap' to Princeton University students most Thursday and Saturday nights."

Q "Generally, **students don't venture off campus to go to bars and clubs**. Sometimes we'll go into New York, but there really isn't much in the town. The ones that are there are very strict about IDs, but once you're legal, some kids do go to Triumph or another bar called Ivy Inn."

Q "I've never been to any bars or clubs. **Most people don't go because of the eating club system.** They function kind of like frats—most eating clubs are on tap Thursday, Friday, and Saturday nights, and a few will always be open to anyone with Princeton ID. There's little reason to go to bars or clubs off campus. They have free beer, and sometimes they have better stuff if a club is having something like margarita night. Plus, there's also always some kind of entertainment like a live band or a DJ. Not too many bars exist; there are only about three in town and no clubs. I guess the most popular bar is Triumph Brewery."

Q "It's pretty weird. Since Princeton is in a New Jersey suburb, **there's really nothing to do off campus**, except go to the movies, malls, and some restaurants. Coming from a city, it's been a difficult transition."

Q "The whole party scene revolves around the eating clubs. Some are selective, meaning that there's an interview process to get in (we call that process 'bicker,' while others are 'sign-in,' meaning you sign up and you're in the club. Each club has its own personality. The big party nights are Thursday and Saturday (people do their own thing on Fridays). Clubs will have DJs, bands, formal dances, etc. You can walk in to any of the sign in clubs, but most of the bicker clubs require passes. **The scene gets old pretty quickly**, but when there's nothing else to do, you learn to deal. Princeton is completely dead as a town, but New York City is an hour away."

The College Prowler Take On...
Nightlife

Princeton hardly has a dozen of social options available, but between the Street, room parties, the bars of Nassau Street, and convenient transportation to both New York and Philadelphia, options exist. While the average night out at Princeton's clubs and bars tends to be quite average, signature, legendary Princeton "holidays," such as Newman's Day and Dean's Date, which encourage late nights out, more than make up for a somewhat monotonous social scene. Annual special events hosted by the eating clubs, including Houseparties and Winter Formals, provide a nice break from just going out.

For most students, the Street gets old by the end of sophomore year. They have bickered or signed in or gone independent and start looking for more options. Fortunately, by the end of sophomore year, most students are on the brink of 21 and can start going to Princeton's bars, which will keep them entertained for a few more weeks. By junior year, Princeton students begin to immerse themselves in their independent work, so visiting the Street becomes somewhat of a privilege, as the increasingly rigorous academic work does not allow students to spend too much time out and about junior and senior years. Despite the proximity of New York and Philadelphia, public transportation is somewhat inflexible, as the last train on a Saturday night leaves New York Penn Station around 1 a.m., leaving students stranded in Princeton Junction unless they are willing to pay the hefty late night cab fare.

The College Prowler™ Grade on
Nightlife: C

A high grade in Nightlife indicates that there are many bars and clubs in the area that are easily accessible and affordable. Other determining factors include the number of options for the under-21 crowd and the prevalence of house parties.

Greek Life

The Lowdown On...
Greek Life

Number of Fraternities:
14

Number of Sororities:
4

Percent of Undergrad Men in Fraternities:
20%

Percent of Undergrad Women in Sororities:
15%

Multicultural Colonies:
Alpha Epsilon Pi
Delta Sigma Theta
Alpha Kappa Alpha
Lambda Upsilon Lambda
Zeta Phi Beta
Sigma Lambda Upsilon

Fraternities on Campus:

Beta Theta Pi
Chi Phi
Delta Kappa Epsilon
Delta Phi
Delta Psi
Kappa Alpha Order
Phi Kappa Sigma
Pi Kappa Alpha
Sigma Alpha Epsilon
Sigma Chi
Sigma Phi
Theta Delta Chi
Zeta Beta Tau
Zeta Psi

Sororities on Campus:

Delta Delta Delta
Kappa Alpha Theta
Kappa Kappa Gamma
Pi Beta Phi

Other Greek Organizations:

Panhellenic Council

Students Speak Out On...
Greek Life

{ **"Frats and sororities aren't a big part of campus because of 'The Street.' There are some, but they aren't that big because they're not recognized by the University."**

Q "There is a growing presence of the Greek life, although **no houses exist.** The majority of social scene is found at the eating clubs."

Q "Greek life has a **minimal role at Princeton.** I wasn't involved in it at all and rarely saw it, but there are a few sororities and fraternities. The social scene revolves around the eating clubs; Greek life is really minor."

Q "There are fraternities, but **they are not officially recognized by the University.** So, you'll find some dorm frat parties, but the frats are usually strongly linked to one or more of the eating clubs. Most of the social life is dominated by the eating clubs; there is a fair amount of drinking that goes on."

Q "There is Greek life on campus—it is pretty popular although **not absolutely essential to Princeton.** It is growing in popularity. I am in a sorority, and I love it."

Q "Greek life is there, but **not too prevalent.** I'm in a sorority, and I absolutely love it, but social life really revolves around the eating clubs."

Q "Technically, **I guess we have Greek life**, but it's not too big, and the University doesn't acknowledge it. The eating clubs have nearly eradicated the need for Greek life, since being a member is like being in a coed frat. Their parties are usually better than lame, University-run entertainment. They're run by students while the University looks the other way."

Q "There are a **few Greek organizations**, but none of them have houses; they definitely don't dominate the social scene. If you're in one, that's cool, but it's not really a big deal. Greek life is not a big part of the scene. There are frats, but they do not have houses; they are more like social clubs. Eating clubs are where all the parties are; they have free liquor."

The College Prowler Take On...
Greek Life

Princeton University does not officially recognize the fraternities and sororities that exist on campus. Unofficially, the University has been trying for years to figure out whether to incorporate the existing Greek system into campus life or how to rid the campus of any form of Greek system. Fraternities initially started on Princeton's campus in the 1840s, but, fearing the deterioration of Princeton's celebrated debate societies, the administration forbade any Greek presence on campus. To do this, Princeton's administrators required students to sign a pledge that they would not go Greek for the next hundred years. Without houses and without recognition from the University, Princeton's modern Greek system does not have much of a presence on campus and most students are disinterested in the system.

Greek life is somewhat intertwined with the eating club system, particularly in the bicker clubs. The decision to go Greek is one of the first questions students must answer after arriving on campus freshman year. While men chose to rush only one fraternity, women rush all sororities and are almost always guaranteed a bid from at least one. The pledge process for women is extremely tame, whereas, for the majority of fraternities, the pledge process is much more involved. Greek organizations give freshmen and sophomores social options outside of their residential colleges. Greek life can also pave the way for some students into selective bicker clubs. There are no fraternity or sorority houses on or near campus, so the system relies entirely upon room parties and off-campus events, such as formals and tailgates. Greek life does not limit one's group of friends and can serve as a way for normally shy students to open up and meet people outside of their residential college before making the decision sophomore year regarding their eating options.

The College Prowler™ Grade on
Greek Life: C-

Clarification: A good grade means that Greek life has a highly-visible role on campus. The poorer the grade, the less prominent the Greek scene.

Drug Scene

The Lowdown On...
Drug Scene

Most Prevalent Drugs on Campus:

Alcohol

Marijuana

Cocaine

Attention-enhancing drugs (e.g. Ritalin, Dexedrine and Adderall)

Liquor-Related Referrals:

244

Liquor-Related Arrests:

28

Drug-Related Referrals:

22

Drug-Related Arrests:

3

Drug Counseling Programs:

Alcohol and Drug Educators

Services: Provide order-in programs for RA groups; design and circulate flyers, brochures, and other promotional materials; lead discussion groups and workshops for campus organizations and groups; publicize National Alcohol Screening Day; staff information tables; assist in planning outreach activities and programs; act as referral sources for students struggling with substance abuse

Counseling Center Alcohol and Other Drugs Team

Phone: (609) 258-3285

Services: Assessment; short-term individual psychotherapy; support group for students looking to control their drinking; referrals to private therapists, treatment programs and groups; consultation to University staff and faculty members on addressing alcohol problems of students

Students Speak Out On...
Drug Scene

> "The drug scene isn't that bad. Marijuana is the dominant drug. I think very few people do the hardcore drugs."

Q "It's present like at any other university. It depends on the crowd. There is a lot of wealth, so **designer drugs are popular.**"

Q "It's not bad. Of course **they are in circulation**, but it's nothing infringing."

Q "Honestly, I tried to avoid the drug scene and succeeded. I think **it's pretty safe to say that it's there**, but only if you choose to be part of it, although pot is more abundant."

Q "There's some drug use, **mostly pot.** Some harder stuff shows up occasionally, but I don't think it's huge. You can find a drug scene if you're into that. Alcohol dominates."

Q "I'd say there's not really a drug scene. I mean, I would think that there would be some, like at any place you go, but I have **never heard of any bad things in Princeton.** I think I heard of something only once and it had to do with pot. All the drug scenes are in the big cities like Philly, New York, Trenton, and so on."

Q "As far as I can tell, it's pretty small. **There's a fairly large drinking scene**, but as far as drugs go, I'd say it's only among a group of people."

Q "I'm not really sure. **I have never encountered any drug-related issues**."

The College Prowler Take On...
Drug Scene

Like almost any other university, there are drugs present on Princeton's campus. The drug scene on Princeton's campus is not very visible, but it is present. With the strong presence of eating clubs as the main dining and social option for students, alcohol is the source of the majority of strain in the relationship between administrators and students. Each weekend, a number of students have to visit McCosh Health Center, or "get McCosh-ed," for alcohol-related issues. Other than alcohol, marijuana is the most prevalent drug on campus.

Increasingly, a small minority of Princeton students have started to use drugs other than alcohol and marijuana. A recent article in the Daily Princetonian reported an increasing presence of drugs such as cocaine and Aderrall on campus. Because of the academic pressures, some students opt to use prescription drugs, such as Ritalin, to stay awake to do work. Most students at Princeton do not use drugs, and it is by no means a widespread problem.

The College Prowler™ Grade on
Drug Scene: B-

Clarification: A good grade means that drugs are not a highly-visible threat on campus. The poorer the grade, the more prominent the drug scene.

Campus Strictness

The Lowdown On...
Campus Strictness

What Are You Most Likely to Get Caught Doing on Campus?

- Drinking underage
- Drinking in common areas
- Public urination or indecency
- Parking illegally
- Making too much noise in your dorm
- Having candles or other contraband items in your dorm room

Students Speak Out On...
Campus Strictness

"Campus police aren't too strict on drugs and drinking. There are lots of room parties on campus that aren't broken up until things get too loud or out of control. You can pretty much do what you want in your room."

Q "I'll give you a little parable. When I was pre-fresh and came to visit, **I attended a party with a pool filled with beer.** Eh? I mean come on!"

Q "**They're not very strict about drinking**. Just don't walk around with open containers. I don't know about drugs; I never did them and never knew anyone who did."

Q "They're **not very strict,** although it'll probably get stricter, as there have been more incidents in the news."

Q "As long as drinking is done in a manner that doesn't disturb others, and as long as people don't start passing out and calling ambulances, **things are fine**."

Q "Drugs are really not an issue and are pretty unaccepted within the student body, so it's not an issue with police. A lot of drinking goes on, and the **University has been trying to crack down on it recently but with little success.** For people who like to go out, drinking is a large part of the social culture."

Q "**They won't tolerate drugs if they find out.** With drinking, they tend to look the other way unless someone is hospitalized or something. They bust room parties sometimes, but no one is ever arrested. Drinking is a different thing, but campus police will look the other way. They're not strict at all; there are parties outside all the time."

Q "They're **rather relaxed** in nature as long as the students not too loud or obviously breaking rules."

The College Prowler Take On...
Campus Strictness

Few Princeton students will find themselves under the scrutiny of Princeton's campus police or University administration. Those students who do can be called in for any number of reasons, from climbing tent scaffolding at Reunions to breaking into a dining hall after hours to get a scoop of ice cream. Room parties tend to be broken up not because of presumed underage drinking but because of noise complaints. Just as long as those students who chose to drink do so without breaking noise and open container regulations, Public Safety does not give them too much of a problem.

Campus police rely mostly on town police for taking care of major issues. The campus police focus more on problems such as noise complaints, which may result from parties where alcohol is served. The majority of calls to Public Safety are about thefts and alcohol-related issues, such as drunk students needing transport to McCosh Health Center.

The College Prowler™ Grade on

Campus Strictness: B+

Clarification: A good grade means that campus strictness is not overwhelmingly present. The poorer the grade, the more strict the campus.

Parking

The Lowdown On...
Parking

Student Parking Lot?
Yes

Freshman Allowed to Park?
No

Approximate Parking Permit Cost:
$135/year for automobiles, $50/year for mopeds

Princeton Parking Services:

(609) 258-3157

Department of Public Safety, A-Level, New South Hall

web.princeton.edu/sites/publicsafety/Parking.htm

Parking Permits:

Starting with the Class of 2007, freshmen are not allowed to bring cars to school. Most undergrads who apply for parking permits get them. There are two student parking lots: one far from the main part of campus near Jadwin Gym and the other one slightly closer between the main part of campus and Lake Carnegie. To apply, students should go to the Parking Office in New South before the end of the academic year to obtain a pass for the upcoming year. The earlier a student applies, the most likely he or she is to get a space in the closer lot.

Best Places to Find a Parking Spot:

Lot 23

Good Luck Getting a Parking Spot Here:

As long as you apply for a space early enough, no parking space in a student lot is unobtainable.

Common Parking Tickets:

Violations (e.g. parking outside of designated areas, parking without a valid decal, parking outside of a designated space): $20

Late penalty after 10 days: $10

Booting/Towing (plus all outstanding charges): $ 60

Vehicles WITH decals will be booted/towed when in noncompliance with boot/tow Regulations. Cars parked in violation WITHOUT a University parking decal will be warned and (if no response) booted or towed.

Students Speak Out On...
Parking

> **"Parking sucks because there aren't a lot of places you can park without incurring a $20 fine. There are a few big lots where everyone parks, but these are generally pretty far from the living areas."**

Q "Parking is not really a problem, but **the lot is relatively far from your dorm**, so it's always kind of a big deal to go get your car for something. There's only temporary parking near the dorms. A lot of students don't have cars because you don't really need to go off campus if you don't want to."

Q "Parking for freshman is pretty far, but **it's available.** It gets better as you get older."

Q "There is **plenty of parking,** buts it is rather inconvenient. Parking anywhere other than in designated areas will result in getting towed."

Q "**It's not bad.** There are numerous lots to park in just for students."

Q "Parking is **somewhat easy.** Everyone gets a space, but sometimes its far-ish, depending on where you live."

Q "Parking is usually five minutes from your room at best, 15 -20 minutes away at worst. **I highly advocate getting a bike.** I've seen little need for cars on campus."

Q "Mainly everything is within walking distance in Princeton, so you really don't need to drive anywhere. **There is parking—and a lot of it**—mainly around the pool and gym. There is room; you just might have to walk a little to get to your class, because the classes are kind of far away from the parking."

Q "It's **not that hard to park**. All you have to do is register the first day you get here, and there shouldn't be a problem."

Q "The parking lot is about a **10 - 15 minute walk from the dorms.** Parking on the street is kind of difficult, though, because the town is always crowded, and there's only parallel metered parking on the streets. I have my car and it's definitely worth it."

The College Prowler Take On...
Parking

One major strength in Princeton's parking program is that it is possible to walk nearly everywhere on campus, so parking is a non-issue. There are plenty of restaurants, shops, and small groceries within walking distance of the dorms. For independent students who need a wider selection of food, the Undergraduate Student Government has organized a free grocery delivery service. When students need to go off-campus, there are plenty of shuttle buses between the dorms and parking lots throughout the day.

It is possible to walk everywhere in the town of Princeton. For those who are not so energetic to walk to distant parking lots to pick up their cars, a campus shuttle runs throughout campus. While the shuttle bus runs regularly through most of the day, the parking lots are far from campus security booths. The lots all have lights and campus security blue phones, but they can be intimidating during certain times of day. That said, crime in the parking lots is rare, but it would be a good idea to carry a cell phone at the very least.

The College Prowler™ Grade on
Parking: B

A high grade in this section indicates that parking is both available and affordable, and that parking enforcement isn't overly severe.

Transsportation

The Lowdown On...
Transportation

Ways to Get Around Town:
On Campus

Campus Shuttle, 5 p.m.-10:40 p.m., (609) 258-6861

Dial-a-Ride, 10:40 p.m.-2 a.m., (609) 258-6861

Tiger Tram, 5:30 a.m.-6:45 p.m.

Public Transportation:
Buses

The 605 route runs between the Princeton Shopping Center on N. Harrison Street and the major malls (including Quaker Bridge) on Route 1. To go from campus to the malls, wait on Palmer Square or at the bus stop in front of Forbes College. Fare is $1 (drivers do not make change). To go from campus to the Princeton Shopping Center, wait in front of Nassau Hall or at the bus stop next to the Dinky Station. The fare is the same.

→

(Buses, continued)

The 606 route runs from the Princeton Shopping Center on North Harrison Street, along Nassau Street, then south on U.S. 206 to downtown Trenton and its eastern suburbs. Stops include the Lawrenceville School, Rider University, the New Jersey State Capitol, New Jersey State Library, and New Jersey State Museum, and many Mercer County government offices. This bus line also connects in downtown Trenton to most other bus lines in the county. To take the 606 to Trenton, wait at the Palmer Square kiosk. Fare to Rider University is $1.40 each way; to downtown Trenton it is $1.70 each way, exact amount required. Transfers are an additional $.40. Approximate time to downtown Trenton is 30-35 minutes.

Trains

The Dinky, a two-car shuttle train run by New Jersey Transit, connects Princeton and Princeton Junction. The Dinky station is located across University Place from McCarter Theatre and is adjacent to the WaWa. The Dinky schedule can be found on-line at New Jersey Transit's website, http://www. njtransit.com.

Taxi Cabs

A-1 Princeton Taxi Inc., (609) 921-1177

A Noble Limousine, (609) 490-1122, (609) 921-0030

A Princeton Taxicab, (609) 924-7300

A Princeton Taxi, (609) 497-9022

Associated Taxi Stand, (609) 924-1222

Attaché Limousine Service, (609) 924-7029, (888) 924-7055 (toll-free)

Car Rentals

Avis, local: (609) 924-4100, (609) 452-8285; national: (800) 831-2847, www.avis.com

Budget, local: (609) 882-2661; national: (800) 527-0700, www.budget.com

Hertz, local: (609) 452-9548; national: (800) 654-3131, www.hertz.com

Best Ways to Get Around Town:

Because Princeton is so small, it is fastest to walk around town. If going to a particularly distant point, such as the Engineering Quad or one of the student parking lots, a bike is recommended.

Ways to Get Out of Town:

Airports:

JFK International Airport, (718) 244-4444

- JFK is primarily a Manhattan airport and is not as accessible as Newark Airport.

How to Get There:

N.J. Transit offers a shuttle train, known locally as the "Dinky," between campus (across from McCarter Theatre) and Princeton Junction. At Princeton Junction, you may transfer to N.J. Transit's Northeast Corridor line northbound. Debark the train at New York Penn Station and take the A or E subway to the airport. The total cost is $11.80 each way. There are also shuttle buses that run between New York Penn Station and JFK for about $15 each way. Alternatively, for a few more dollars, you can pick up the Airporter at Dillon Gym for $36 each way with only a transfer at Newark Airport.

A Cab Ride to the Airport Costs: $120 per car, plus tolls, parking and gratuity

LaGuardia International Airport, (718) 533-3400

- LaGuardia is primarily a Manhattan airport and is not as accessible as Newark Airport.

How to Get There: N.J. Transit offers a shuttle train, known locally as the "Dinky," between campus (across from McCarter Theatre) and Princeton Junction. At Princeton Junction, you may transfer to N.J. Transit's Northeast Corridor line northbound. Debark the train at New York Penn Station and take New York Airport Service Express Bus or SuperShuttle to LaGuardia. The total cost is $19.80 (New York Airport Service Express Bus) or $23.30 (SuperShuttle).

A Cab Ride to the Airport Costs: $125 per car, plus tolls, parking and gratuity

Newark Liberty International Airport, (973) 961-6000

- Newark Airport is 40 miles and approximately 45 minutes driving time from Princeton.

How to Get There: N.J. Transit offers a shuttle train, known locally as the "Dinky," between campus (across from McCarter Theatre) and Princeton Junction. At Princeton Junction, you may transfer to N.J. Transit's Northeast Corridor line northbound. Debark the train at Newark Liberty International Airport and transfer to the AirTrain monorail. Alternatively, for a few more dollars, you can pick up the Airporter at Dillon Gym for $19 each way.

A Cab Ride to the Airport Costs: $75 per car, plus tolls, parking and gratuity

Philadelphia International Airport, (215) 937-6937

- Philadelphia International Airport is 55 miles and about an hour driving time from Princeton.

How to Get There: Take N.J. Transit train from Princeton (Dinky) Station to Princeton Junction. Transfer to the Northeast Corridor line southbound, which will end in two stops at Trenton station. Transfer to the SEPTA R7 train to Philadelphia 30th Street Station. Take SEPTA R1 train from 30th Street to the airport. Alternatively, take the Dinky to Princeton Junction and take an Amtrak to Philadelphia 30th Street Station before picking up the SEPTA R1 train. The total cost is about $16.15.

A Cab Ride to the Airport Costs: $79 per car, plus parking and gratuity

Amtrak

The Amtrak Train Station is in Princeton Junction, which is accessible by N.J. Transit's Princeton Dinky shuttle. For schedule information, call (800) 872-7245.

http://www.amtrak.com

2 Wallace Rd.

Princeton Junction, NJ 08550

Travel Agents

AAA Travel, 3495 US Highway 1, Princeton, (609) 419-1704

American Express One, 10 Nassau St., Princeton, (609) 921-3888

Edwards Travel, 10 S. Tulane St., Princeton, (609) 924-4443

Empress Travel Agency, 3371 US Highway 1, # 168, Lawrenceville, (609) 987-0580

Liberty Travel, 171 Quaker Bridge Mall, Lawrenceville, (609) 799-8666

Students Speak Out On...
Transportation

> "The train actually runs through Princeton's campus, so it is pretty convenient for getting to New York City or the rest of New Jersey. It also connects to Amtrak should you want to go further. It was very convenient."

Q "It's the best. **You can get anywhere you need to go.** There are trains, buses, and cabs."

Q "There's **great train transportation to New York City**, Philly etc. The train station is right on campus."

Q "Public transportation is **pretty good.** There is a train station on campus (The Dinky) that connects directly to the main New Jersey Transit train line. The Princeton Airporter also comes right on campus for transportation to the airport, and there are campus shuttles that go to the grocery store. The buses are pretty good, too. You can probably get pretty much anywhere in the state on public transportation."

Q "I don't know about the buses because I never take them, and taxis are not big in New Jersey. **The trains, however, in my opinion, are great**; they have the New Jersey Transit, which takes you right to New York and stops along the way. Then they have Amtrak, which takes you everywhere, pretty much. There is this other new, super train that takes you up to Boston in half the time that it would take any other train to get there. Of course you also have the airports."

Q "**It's all very convenient.** New Jersey transit trains stop literally on the edge of the campus. For $16, you can go between Princeton and New York City without using a car."

Q "There are **buses that run through Princeton** and will take you out to Route 1 (the nearest main highway) where you can go to stores like Target and Wal-Mart."

Q "The only public transportation I ever took here was the 605 bus, which goes to Wal-Mart. **It costs a dollar each way and leaves every hour.** Typically, you won't need public transportation because you won't go off campus that much. New Jersey Transit has a train that comes to campus. You can get to New York's Penn Station in a little over an hour. It's pretty convenient."

The College Prowler Take On...
Transportation

When Princeton students venture off campus, they can get almost anywhere by bus, air, or train. For a weekend in Boston, for example, students can choose between taking New Jersey Transit to New York City and then taking one of the popular Chinatown buses, flying on a shuttle between one of the Manhattan airports and Logan Airport, and taking Amtrak straight to Boston. A weekend in Washington yields just as many options. For everyday errands, the New Jersey Transit bus system links Princeton to several area malls and super centers.

Princeton's public transportation is very accessible, but it is somewhat inconvenient for students. The train connecting Princeton and Princeton Junction runs only once an hour through most of the day and stops running for several hours during the night, which puts huge constraints on nights out in New York City. There are plenty of airport options, which allows students to comparison shop for airline tickets home and for vacations. Several mechanical problems on the rail system have created unfortunate delays, but that can be expected on almost any system.

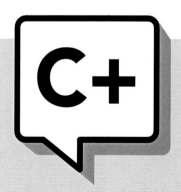

The College Prowler™ Grade on

Transportation: C+

A high grade for Transportation indicates that campus buses, public buses, cabs and rental cars are readily available and affordable. Other determining factors include proximity to an airport and the necessity of transportation.

Weather

The Lowdown On...
Weather

Average Temperature
Fall: 54°F
Winter: 32°F
Spring: 50°F
Summer: 72°F

Average Precipitation
Fall: 3.79"
Winter: 3.41"
Spring: 4.1"
Summer: 4.59"

Students Speak Out On...
Weather

{ **"Fall at Princeton is the best. The leaves turn lots of beautiful colors, and the air is so crisp. It is great weather for IM sports and sitting in front of the fire at your club."**

Q "The weather is pretty crappy. It is hot and humid in the summertime and cold and snowy in the winter. **The worst thing is that the weather is insanely inconsistent.** It will be 80 degrees one week and snowing the next. It's also different every year. Generally, it's very warm in September and October, and it cools down a lot in the winter. Spring may or may not happen, and then it becomes really hot and muggy."

Q "It's **New Jersey weather**. It's all similar on the East Coast."

Q "When it's cold, it's cold! **But it's still beautiful!** I have no complaints. However, when it is nice … it's indescribable!"

Q "I turned my thesis in April 8, and there was snow on the ground. The year before, seniors got to sit outside in swimsuits when they were done. Basically, **the weather is inconsistent at best.**"

Q "The weather is **so gorgeous in the fall.** There is nothing prettier than a bike ride around Carnegie Lake when the leaves are turning. It's cold in the winter. Spring is awesome. It's gorgeous, fun, and just a huge outdoor celebration."

Q "**Spring is the best season at Princeton.** You can use your meals to get a barbeque from the dining hall, and there are plenty of grassy areas where you can sit out and get some sun while you read. Princeton is kind of like a country club in that you can go for a swim at the pool and then play a friendly match of tennis down at the campus courts."

Q "It **rains fairly frequently.** Summers can be very hot and humid, and winters can get cold. Most winters it snows. I guess 'seasonal' is the best way to really describe it."

Q "Fortunately, few students stick around for summer. **New Jersey gets hazy, hot, and humid**, and Scully is the only air-conditioned dorm."

Q "Even if it snows a foot, don't expect a day off of class. It won't happen. **Princeton cancelled class once last year for a blizzard.** It was the first time class had been cancelled in decades."

Q "The **weather is always changing.** It's hot and humid in the summer and cold and rainy in the winter. The East Coast is cold. I really like the different seasons. It's nice to have a break from the same old thing, although it really does get cold in the winter."

Q "We have **all four seasons**—you have summer, fall, winter and spring. It gets kind of depressing in the winter, to tell you the truth, but when the sun comes out in the spring, it's all good again."

The College Prowler Take On...
Weather

Princeton definitely has four seasons: a crisp fall, chilly winter, rainy spring, and humid summer. With only one air-conditioned dorm on campus and self-regulated heating just as much of a rarity, students are constantly aware of weather conditions. The weather in Princeton is somewhat schizophrenic. While the changes in season are somewhat predictable, New Jersey weather is notorious for its unexpected shifts and surprises. For example, a hurricane socked the East Coast on the first day of classes, and the University went to stringent water restrictions shortly thereafter. Showers were strictly forbidden, and laundry rooms around campus were closed. Weather like that left many of the new freshmen wondering why they had picked Princeton, but it really served as a bonding experience for students, who came up with dozens of jokes starting, "If it's yellow...."

By the time school starts in September, it is hot for about a week and then quickly cools down. Most of the dorms and classrooms do not have A/C, so it is essential to pack comfortable clothing and several fans. Because many of the dorms are so old, some students prefer to live on lower floors on the theory that heat rises. Once the hazy, hot, and humid days are gone, the weather stays warm into the fall, which is generally crisp and cool. The fall foliage stirs up images of long walks on the golf course and along Lake Carnegie. By December, it is so cold that you cannot remember September's Indian summer. It does not snow much at Princeton, but, when it does, it is important to have the appropriate clothing, because students walk everywhere. By March, it starts to warm up again, at which point it will rain for a few weeks. By the end of the school year, it gets hot again, and it is necessary to bring fans out of storage. Spring at Princeton is a time for getting some sun and outdoor relaxation.

B-

The College Prowler™ Grade on
Weather: B-

A high Weather grade designates that temperatures are mild and rarely reach extremes, that the campus tends to be sunny rather than rainy, and that weather is fairly consistent rather than unpredictable.

Overall Experience

Students Speak Out On...
Overall Experience

{ **"I love it here. It's a little conservative, but the opportunities are fabulous. I love Princeton and have had incredible experiences."**

Q "Princeton is a great place, but it's definitely not for everybody. My experience, overall, has been pretty good. It's not the perfect place for me, but I don't think that any college is perfect for anyone. Again, **Princeton is not for everybody.** Princeton is the kind of place that should be totally amazing but somehow is not. There is a weird vibe, but it also completely depends on who you know, where you end up, and what kind of person you are because most people love it."

Q "My overall experience has been **very positive**. Initially, like many others, I wasn't that thrilled with the school because it is very much a closed campus, and there's not tremendous choice in terms of the social scene. But, freshman year, **I made some really close friends** with people in my hallway, and from there, I started to like it more and more. You get used to the uniqueness of the school. I got involved in sports and had a great time. The four years have gone so fast, and I'm actually a little sad that it's time to move on."

Q "It is **impossible to love every second at Princeton,** because the work is simply too demanding. In the midst of all of the work, however, you will make some of the strongest bonds of your life, whether it is with professors, graduate students, administrators, support staff, or your fellow students. The Princeton bond is not limited to just that population either. Alumni are more than willing to share their wealth of knowledge and experience with students so that they can get the best opportunities in the workplace. A friend of mine networked during his sophomore year and got an offer for a paid internship at one of the country's top investment banks before his junior year, a year earlier than the official recruitment process even begins!"

Q "Princeton has challenged me in ways that I could have never imagined. My first obstacle was the freshman-year roommate who kept weird hours and who I could find clacking away on her computer keyboard while I was trying to sleep. The next obstacle was finding ways to make the meals in the dining hall bearable, but the reward of good eating club food was totally worth it. While my intro level courses were difficult, it was a different kind of difficult from the upper level ones. Whereas my intro level courses were a challenge to my academic endurance, the upper level ones always left me thinking. In the end, **it was a privilege to get to work with some of the greatest minds and most influential people of our time.**"

Q "Princeton people are **amazing and non-competitive**— I've had people pull all-nighters with me just to help me pass my exams. Princeton is a place where your major concern is what's going on around campus. There are always tons of things going on, but the University is all about the undergrads. I always felt that I was at school to learn and grow and that I could focus on whatever I wanted. It really has been amazing."

Q "I found the pre-med process at Princeton very frustrating. **The people in my required courses were extremely competitive.** It took me a few semesters to find a group of other students who felt the same way who were willing to work together to make it through the tough intro level courses like orgo."

Q "I loved Princeton so much that **I found it difficult to maintain friendships from high school**, because my old friends simply did not understand the combination of the rigorous academic program with the fantastic social life. They could not look beyond what they thought as Princeton's nerdy students to see some of the most dynamic people I have ever known."

Q "When I describe my college experience to other people, **I say it is sort of like summer camp.** You go through many intense emotions that you have never experienced before and wonder if other people feel the same way. Once you realize that you are not alone, you become inseparable from these people."

Q "I've **loved every minute of my years here.** The people are amazing and the academics are so interesting. There is every activity imaginable, and it is just such an amazing place. Choosing Princeton was the best decision I've ever made."

Q "I love Princeton. If you have the opportunity, **come to school here.**"

Palmer Inn (Best Western)

www.bestwestern.com

3499 U.S. Route 1

Princeton, NJ

(609) 452-2500,
(800) 688-0500

Distance from Campus:
3 miles

Price Range: $100-$150
(includes breakfast buffet)

Red Roof Inn

www.redroof.com

3203 U.S. Route 1

Lawrenceville

(609) 896-3388,
(800) 843-7663

Distance from Campus:
6 miles

Price Range: $65.99
(weekday), $69.99 (weekend)

Take a Campus Virtual Tour

www.princeton.edu/~okkey/tourstart.html

To Schedule a Group Information Session or Interview:

Call (609) 258-3060 on any weekday. During the summer, hours are from 8:30 a.m.-4:30 p.m., and hours are 9 a.m.-5 p.m. for the rest of the year.

Interviews are not a required part of the admission process, but campus visits are highly encouraged by the Admissions staff. From May through December, applicants can schedule appointments to meet with members of the Admission staff. Such appointments may include up to six applicants.

To Schedule an Alumni Interview:

From October through February, students who have submitted an application for admission may be contacted by a Princeton Alumni Schools Committee (ASC) member, depending upon the student's location and the availability of a committee member in that area. Recently, over seventy percent of applicants in any given year have met with a member of the ASC.

To Schedule a General Information Session:

Call (609) 258-3060 on any weekday from April through January. During those months, there is a daily information session at 12:30 p.m.

Interested students and parents are welcome to these daily information sessions, which are conducted by an admission office. The sessions run approximately an hour in length.

Campus Tours:

Campus tours run daily, except University Holidays, including Labor Day Weekend. The student-led Orange Key Tours last about an hour and depart from the Welcome Desk at the Frist Campus Center. From Monday through Saturday, tours depart at 10 a.m., 11 a.m., 1:30 p.m., and 3:30 p.m. On Sundays, tours leave at 1:30 p.m. and 3:30 p.m. Call in advance of your visit to check the availability of the tour!

Overnight Visits:

Princeton has an accepted students weekend each April, commonly called Pre-Frosh Weekend. Accepted students have the opportunity to sleep in a dorm room and are paired with underclassmen, so they have the chance to attend classes, eat in the dining halls, and experience residential college life. Usually, the eating clubs go off-tap for the weekend, so pre-frosh don't get an accurate portrayal of Princeton's social life.

DIRECTIONS TO CAMPUS

Driving from the North:

- Take the New Jersey Turnpike south to Exit 9 (New Brunswick).
- After the toll booths, take the first right turn onto the ramp for Route 18 north.
- Soon after you enter Route 18, take the left side of a fork in the road, staying in the right lane.
- Immediately bear right for an exit to U.S. Route 1 south/ Trenton.
- Drive south on Route 1 for about 18 miles to the Alexander Road exit and follow signs for Princeton.
- At Faculty Road (traffic light, gas station) turn right, and proceed to the traffic circle.
- Go three quarters of the way around the circle and turn right onto Elm Drive.
- At the next traffic circle, go half-way around and proceed to the traffic kiosk.

Driving from the South:

- If you are coming from southern New Jersey, take Interstate 295 north (instead of the New Jersey Turnpike), exiting at Route 1 north (exit 67).
- Travel about three miles north on Route 1 to the Alexander Road exit, and follow signs for Princeton.
- At Faculty Road (traffic light, gas station) turn right, and proceed to the traffic circle.
- Go three quarters of the way around the circle and turn right onto Elm Drive.
- At the next traffic circle, go half-way around and proceed to the traffic kiosk.

Driving from the East:

- Take Interstate 195 west (toward Trenton) to the exit for Interstate 295 north.
- Drive seven miles to the exit for Route 1 north (exit 67).
- Travel about three miles north on Route 1 to the Alexander Road exit, and follow signs for Princeton.
- At Faculty Road (traffic light, gas station) turn right, and proceed to the traffic circle.
- Go three quarters of the way around the circle and turn right onto Elm Drive.
- At the next traffic circle, go half-way around and proceed to the traffic kiosk.

Driving from the West:

- Drive east on Interstate 78 into New Jersey.
- Exit onto southbound Interstate 287 (toward Somerville).
- Follow signs for Routes 202/206 south.
- Go south on 202 for a short distance and then follow signs to 206 south, which will take you around a traffic circle.
- Go south on 206 for about 18 miles to Nassau Street (Route 27) in the center of Princeton.
- Turn left onto Nassau Street, and follow it to the third traffic light.
- Turn right onto Washington Road.
- Travel down the hill to the light at Faculty Road, and turn right.
- Proceed to the traffic circle, go a quarter of the way around it, and turn right onto Elm Drive.
- At the next traffic circle, go half-way around and proceed to the traffic kiosk.

Words to Know

Academic Probation – A student can receive this if they fail to keep up with their school's academic minimums. Those who are unable to improve their grades after receiving this warning can possibly face dismissal.

Beer Pong / Beirut – A drinking game with numerous cups of beer arranged in a particular pattern on each side of a table. The goal is to get a ping pong ball into one of the opponent's cups by throwing the ball or hitting it with a paddle. If the ball lands in a cup, the opponent is required to drink the beer.

Bid – An invitation from a fraternity or sorority to pledge their specific house.

Blue-Light Phone – Brightly-colored phone posts with a blue light bulb on top. These phones exist for security purposes and are located at various outside locations around most campuses. If a student has an emergency or is feeling endangered, they can pick up one of these phones (free of charge) to connect with campus police or an escort service.

Campus Police – Policemen who are specifically assigned to a given institution. Campus police are not regular city officers; they are employed by the university in a full-time capacity.

Club Sports – A level of sports that falls somewhere between varsity and intramural. If a student is unable to commit to a varsity team but has a lot of passion for athletics, a club sport could be a better, less intense option. If a club sport still requires too much commitment, intramurals often involve no traveling and a lot less time.

Cocaine – An illegal drug. Also known as "coke" or "blow," cocaine often resembles a white crystalline or powdery substance. It is highly addictive and dangerous.

Common Application – An application that students can use to apply to multiple schools.

Course Registration – The time when a student selects what courses they would like for the upcoming quarter or semester. Prior to registration, it is best to have an idea of several back-up courses in case a particular class becomes full. If a course is full, a student can place themselves on the waitlist, although this still does not guarantee entry.

Division Athletics – Athletics range from Division I to Division III. Division IA is the most competitive, while Division III is considered to be the least competitive.

Dorm – Short for dormitory, a dorm is an on-campus housing facility. Dorms can provide a range of options from suite-style rooms to more communal options that include shared bathrooms. Most first-year students live in dorms. Some upperclassmen who wish to stay on campus also choose this option.

Early Action – A way to apply to a school and get an early acceptance response without a binding commitment. This is a system that is becoming less and less available.

Early Decision – An option that students should use only if they are positive that a place is their dream school. If a student applies to a school using the early decision option and is admitted, they are required and bound to attend that university. Admission rates are usually higher with early decision students because the school knows that a student is making them their first choice.

Ecstasy – An illegal drug. Also known as "E" or "X," ecstasy looks like a pill and most resembles an aspirin. Considered a party drug, ecstasy is very dangerous and can be deadly.

Ethernet – An extremely fast internet connection that is usually available in most university-owned residence halls. To use an Ethernet connection properly, a student will need a network card and cable for their computer.

Fake ID – A counterfeit identification card that contains false information. Most commonly, students get fake IDs and change their birthdates so that they appear to be older than 21 (of legal drinking age). Even though it is illegal, many college students have fake IDs in hopes of purchasing alcohol or getting into bars.

Frosh – Slang for "freshmen."

Hazing – Initiation rituals that must be completed for membership into some fraternities or sororities. Numerous universities have outlawed hazing due to its degrading or dangerous requirements.

Sports (IMs) – A popular, and usually free, student activity where students create teams and compete against other groups for fun. These sports vary in competitiveness and can include a range of activities—everything from billiards to water polo. IM sports are a great way to meet people with similar interests.

Keg – Officially called a half barrel, a keg contains roughly 200 12-ounce servings of beer and is often found at college parties.

LSD – An illegal drug. Also known as acid, this hallucinogenic drug most commonly resembles a tab of paper.

Marijuana – An illegal drug. Also known as weed or pot; besides alcohol, marijuana is one of the most commonly-found drugs on campuses across the country.

Major –The focal point of a student's college studies; a specific topic that is studied for a degree. Examples of majors include physics, English, history, computer science, economics, business, and music. Many students decide on a specific major before arriving on campus, while others are simply "undecided" and figure it out later. Those who are extremely interested in two areas can also choose to double major.

Meal Block – The equivalent of one meal. Students on a "meal plan" usually receive a fixed number of meals per week. Each meal, or "block," can be redeemed at the school's dining facilities in place of cash. More often than not, if a student fails to use their weekly allotment of meal blocks, they will be forfeited.

Minor – An additional focal point in a student's education. Often serving as a compliment or addition to a student's main area of focus, a minor has fewer requirements and prerequisites to fulfill than a major. Minors are not required for graduation from most schools; however some students who want to further explore many different interests choose to have both a major and a minor.

Mushrooms – An illegal drug. Also known as "shrooms," this drug looks like regular mushrooms but are extremely hallucinogenic.

Off-Campus Housing – Housing from a particular landlord or rental group that is not affiliated with the university. Depending on the college, off-campus housing can range from extremely popular to non-existent. Those students who choose to live off campus are typically given more freedom, but they also have to deal with things such as possible subletting scenarios, furniture, and bills. In addition to these factors, rental prices and distance often affect a student's decision to move off campus.

Office Hours – Time that teachers set aside for students who have questions about the coursework. Office hours are a good place for students to go over any problems and to show interest in the subject material.

Pledging – The time after a student has gone through rush, received a bid, and has chosen a particular fraternity or sorority they would like to join. Pledging usually lasts anywhere from one to two semesters. Once the pledging period is complete and a particular student has done everything that is required to become a member, they are considered a brother or sister. If a fraternity or a sorority would decide to "haze" a group of students, these initiation rituals would take place during the pledging period.

Private Institution – A school that does not use taxpayers dollars to help subsidize education costs. Private schools typically cost more than public schools and are usually smaller.

Prof – Slang for "professor."

Public Institution – A school that uses taxpayers dollars to help subsidize education costs. Public schools are often a good value for in-state residents and tend to be larger than most private colleges.

Quarter System (sometimes referred to as the Trimester System) – A type of academic calendar system. In this setup, students take classes for three academic periods. The first quarter usually starts in late September or early October and concludes right before Christmas. The second quarter usually starts around early to mid–January and finishes up around March or April. The last quarter, or "third quarter," usually starts in late March or early April and finishes up in late May or Mid-June. The fourth quarter is summer. The major difference between the quarter system and semester system is that students take more courses but with less coverage.

RA (Resident Assistant) – A student leader who is assigned to a particular floor in a dormitory in order to help to the other students who live there. A RA's duties include ensuring student safety and providing guidance or assistance wherever possible.

Recitation – An extension of a specific course; a "review" session of sorts. Because some classes are so large, recitations offer a setting with fewer students where students can ask questions and get help from professors or TAs in a more personalized environment. As a result, it is common for most large lecture classes to be supplemented with recitations.

Rolling Admissions – A form of admissions. Most commonly found at public institutions, schools with this type of policy continue to accept students throughout the year until their class sizes are met. For example, some schools begin accepting students as early as December and will continue to do so until April or May.

Room and Board – This is typically the combined cost of a university-owned room and a meal plan.

Room Draw/Housing Lottery – A common way to pick on-campus room assignments for the following year. If a student decides to remain in university-owned housing, they are assigned a unique number that, along with seniority, is used to choose their new rooms for the next year.

Rush – The period in which students can meet the brothers

The College Prowler Take On...
Overall Experience

Once students get past the relative isolation of Princeton, they immerse themselves in the multitude of campus academic and social activities, from political and humor publications to debate societies to eating clubs. The academic program is demanding, which students appreciate, and it prepares students for not only the work force but also top-notch graduate schools. The historic buildings and eating clubs give Princeton its own sort of feel that may not mesh well with all students but certainly provide Princeton undergrads with a plethora of traditions and opportunities that are characteristically Princeton.

Princeton is not just a school, it is an experience. Students who take full advantage of what Princeton has to offer have the opportunity to work with some of the most talented professors and scholars in the world on an idyllic campus. They graduate with one of the best undergraduate educations in the country and with all the connections the alumni experience has to offer. Some students may not realize the significance of the Princeton experience until they march on to Elm Drive for their graduating P-Rade, but the majority of students know how special the Princeton experience is by the time they are back from the woods on their pre-frosh Outdoor Action trip.

ABOUT THE AUTHOR:

As a native Princetonian, it has been a privilege to work on this book, and hopefully I have been able to accurately convey my enthusiasm for both town and gown. Growing up in the Princeton area has afforded me both the "townie" and student experience, which few get to have. I initially came to Princeton, like many of my peers, with the intention of going to medical school after graduation. Three semesters of college-level chemistry quickly cured me of that plan, and I graduated from Princeton with an A.B. in history and a certificate in American Studies in June 2003. While at Princeton, I managed the Student Facebook Agency, a member of the campus' Student Agencies, a group formed to encourage entrepreneurship on campus, and was an active member in several campus groups. I hope the shared experiences of those interviewed for this book as well as my own personal insights will help you to make the decision to come to Princeton. It is obviously not an experience for everyone, but grueling hours spent preparing thoughtful, well-researched essays for Dean's Date as well as a university-mandated senior thesis have led me to believe that Princeton provides its graduates with one of the strongest liberal arts educations in the country that effectively prepares its students for both the workplace and graduate school. I welcome any comments or questions about this College Prowler Guide, so please email me at alisonfraser@collegeprowler.com.

Alison Fraser

and sisters of a particular chapter and find out if a given fraternity or sorority is right for them. Rushing a fraternity or a sorority is not a requirement at any school. The goal of rush is to give students who are serious about pledging a feel for what to expect.

Semester System – The most common type of academic calendar system at college campuses. This setup typically includes two semesters in a given school year. The "fall" semester starts around the end of August or early September and finishes right before winter vacation. The "spring" semester usually starts in mid-January and ends around late April or May.

Student Center/Rec Center/Student Union – A common area on campus that often contains study areas, recreation facilities, and eateries. This building is often a good place to meet up with fellow students and is most commonly used as a hangout. Depending on the school, the student center can have a huge role or a non-existent role in campus life.

Student ID – A university-issued photo ID that serves as a student's key to many different functions within an institution. Some schools require students to show these cards in order to get into dorms, libraries, cafeterias, and other facilities. In addition to storing meal plan information, in some cases, a student ID can actually work as a debit card and allow students to purchase things from bookstores or local shops.

Suite – A type of dorm room. Unlike other places that have communal bathrooms that are shared by the entire floor, a suite has a private bathroom. Suite-style dorm rooms can house anywhere from two to ten students.

TA (Teacher's Assistant) – An undergraduate or grad student who helps in some manner with a specific course. In some cases, a TA will teach a class, assist a professor, grade assignments, or conduct office hours.

Undergraduate – A student who is in the process of studying for their Bachelor (college) degree.

Report Card Summary

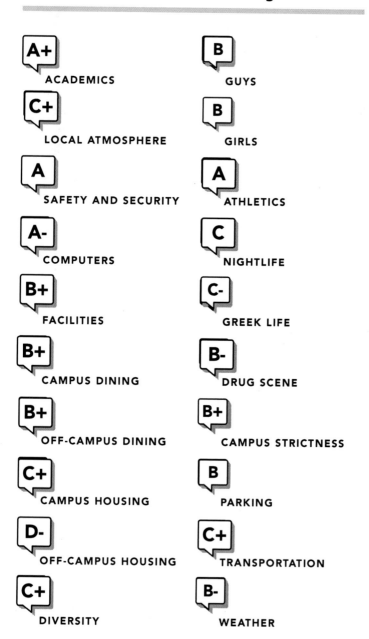

A+
ACADEMICS

C+
LOCAL ATMOSPHERE

A
SAFETY AND SECURITY

A-
COMPUTERS

B+
FACILITIES

B+
CAMPUS DINING

B+
OFF-CAMPUS DINING

C+
CAMPUS HOUSING

D-
OFF-CAMPUS HOUSING

C+
DIVERSITY

B
GUYS

B
GIRLS

A
ATHLETICS

C
NIGHTLIFE

C-
GREEK LIFE

B-
DRUG SCENE

B+
CAMPUS STRICTNESS

B
PARKING

C+
TRANSPORTATION

B-
WEATHER

The Inside Scoop

The Lowdown On...
The Inside Scoop

Princeton Slang:

Know the slang, know the school. The following is a list of things you really need to know before coming to Princeton. The more of these words you know, the better off you'll be.

Academic adviser: The professor your residential college matches you with who will (hopefully) guide you through the stresses of distribution requirements and writing and foreign language requirements

Alexander Beach: Central New Jersey's answer to a beach. The grassy area between Blair, Witherspoon, Alexander, and West College where students sun themselves

Arch sing: Often themed event in either Blair Arch or 1879 Arch during which a cappella groups serenade audiences with some popular songs from their repertoires.

Bicker: The five-day period at the start of second semester during which sophomores wishing to join selective eating clubs go through a rush-like process in order to gain an invitation.

Big Three: Harvard, Princeton, and Yale. Becomes an issue mostly during football season.

Cane Spree: Traditional multi-sport competition held at end of second week of classes between freshmen and sophomores. Central event is cane wrestling between classes.

Cannon Green: Green behind Nassau Hall with cannon partially buried in the center. Location of coveted Big Three bonfire.

Carrel: Cell-like room located all around Firestone Library granted to pairs of seniors to give them a place to store books and other materials for their theses.

CJL: Center for Jewish Life.

Clapper: The part of the Nassau Hall bell that tradition requires the incoming class must capture each year. This tradition came to a halt when a member of the Class of 1995 fell from the bell tower in an attempt to steal the clapper.

Communiversity: Day-long event each April that tries to unify town and gown through activities along Nassau Street and on Nassau Green.

Dean's Date: The last day of reading period when all written course work is due. If a student cannot complete his work, he has to go see a Dean. This is also one of the biggest nights out at the eating clubs.

Dei Sub Numine Viget: Princeton's motto in Latin. Translation: "Under God's Will She Flourishes."

Dinky: Two-car New Jersey train that connects Princeton to Princeton Junction.

Entryway: Section of a dorm or classroom building. Only way to get from one entryway to another is to go outside and back in again.

E-Quad: Engineering Quadrangle.

Fall Break: Week-long vacation at the end of fall-term midterms.

Finals: Three-week period following the end of classes during January and May.

FitzRandolph Gate: Gate in front of Nassau Hall.

Freshman Week: Also called "frosh week." Time for sophomores and upperclassmen to settle in while freshmen attend events organized to help them learn more about campus life.

Frist: Short for Frist Campus Center, the student center.

Hoagie Haven: Also "The Haven." Famed eatery along Nassau Street that stays open late and offers cheap prices.

Honor Code: Princeton institution that is taken very seriously. Student sign a pledge at the end of every paper and exam and are expected to turn in students who they witness cheating.

Hose: Reject from a bicker club.

Houseparties: Three-day party weekend at the end of spring semester. On Friday, students go to a formal, followed by a semi-formal on Saturday, and then Lawnparties on Sunday.

Independent: Upperclassman who is not a member of an eating club, University dining hall, or co-op.

JP: Short for junior paper, the independent paper to be completed by all A.B. students. Some A.B. departments only mandate one JP while others ask for two during the course of junior year.

Kiosk: Security booths at the top and bottom of Elm Drive. Drivers must obtain a parking permit here before being permitted to drive onto campus.

Lake Carnegie: Five mile man-made lake at the bottom of campus. Gift of Andrew Carnegie so that Princeton could have a crew team. Ironically, the boathouse was given by fellow a Pittsburgher.

McCarter Theatre: Theater across University Place from the Dinky station. Hosts Triangle Club shows, public concerts, film series, and plays.

McCosh Hall: Major classroom facility for A.B. students.

Newman's Day: Popular student "holiday," April 24. Participating students try to drink 24 beers in 24 hours without going to sleep, vomiting, or missing class.

Nude Olympics: Now-banned tradition. The tradition dictated that sophomores would participate in naked frolicking in Holder courtyard during the first snowfall of the year.

Old Nassau: Nickname for Princeton University and title of Princeton's alma mater, which is sung at most campus events.

P/D/F: Short for Pass/D/Fail. Students are given four P/D/Fs to use during the course of their Princeton education. They can only use one at a time and must pay attention to the strict deadlines associated with this option.

P-rade: Annual procession of alumni down Elm Drive during Reunions.

Precept: Weekly mandatory supplement to lecture courses to go over problem sets, assignments, and readings. Led by professors or graduate students.

Proctor: Public Safety officer.

Prospect 11: Popular campus drinking challenge. Students must drink a beer at each of the eating clubs during the course of a night.

Prox: Also called PUID, short for Princeton University ID. Allows students to unlock doors into dormitories, charge purchases at the Frist Campus Center, and gain admission to the library, athletic events, and eating clubs.

RA: Abbreviation for Resident Adviser, a junior or senior who helps freshmen get acclimated to life at Princeton

Reading period: Week-and-a-half period at the end of classes for students to work on independent work and catch up on reading before exams.

Reunions: Weekend before commencement when alumni gather on campus for activities such as the P-rade. Famous for its widespread consumption of Budweiser beer under class tents.

Room draw: Computerized lottery that assigns draw times to students for picking rooms each spring for the following academic year. Students have tried for years to figure out how the draw is "randomized" with little success.

Suite: Common type of room on campus that at the very least includes a common room and two bedrooms. Some of the larger ones, which may house up to eleven students, have nicknames such as "The Zoo," "The Kitchen Suite," and "The Cuckoo's Nest."

Thesis: The biggest killjoy for each senior class until the spring deadline. All A.B. students must complete a senior thesis. While some engineering students may avoid a traditional thesis, they will not get past mandatory independent work. For most seniors, finishing thesis work becomes the major activity of their last spring break.

U-Store: Abbreviation for University Store, the campus bookstore. Even though it claims to be unaffiliated with the University, the U-Store is the only place where students can find the few rare appliances that are approved by the Fire Safety Code.

Wa: Short for the WaWa Food Market.

'zees: Short for advisees, the freshmen in an RA group. There are usually groups of approximately 15 to 20 'zees for each RA.

Things I Wish I Knew Before Coming to Princeton

- Get on the smallest meal plan possible.

- Unless you like living in a cave, you should bring several lamps.

- Outdoor and Community Action programs really are a great way to meet people and learn about Princeton while doing something fun and/or useful.

- The U-Store will give you the lowest price on a textbook. For example, you can bring a listing from Barnes and Noble including the cost of shipping, and the U-Store will match your price.

- Opportunities are available as long as you seek them out and talk to people.

- Walking to review sessions in January will make you colder than you have ever felt before. Pack warm clothes!

- Meet as many people as possible during Freshman Week.

- Cinderblocks are essential in a small dorm room.

Tips to Succeed at Princeton

- Use all resources that are available to pick your classes— RAs, Student Course Guide—and do not believe everything your academic advisor says.

- Pick classes you actually like.

- Take advantage of as many special lecture series as possible.

- Research your professors before choosing your classes.

- Go to class. Never miss precept.

- Check your e-mail constantly, but do not spend all your time on the Internet.

- Ask the TAs tons of questions.

- Try to complete your distribution requirements as early as possible. If you can't find a class you want to take in a given semester that fills a distribution requirement, look at the Bulletin to see if something more interesting is going to be offered the following semester.

- Actually use reading period, and go to all review sessions.

Urban Legends

- A curse placed on the University when it was originally founded brought bad luck and death to all of the University presidents, which is why there were so many presidents in Princeton's first years.

- Butler College was designed in such a depressing manor to remind students of the horrors of the Holocaust, which explains the barbed-wire-esque structures atop each of the buildings.

- The eating clubs were formed to promote better understanding of gourmet food amongst the uncouth Princeton men.

- James Buchanan Duke offered Princeton a large sum of money in the 1920s to change its name to Duke. When the University refused, he donated the money instead to Trinity College in North Carolina, which is why Duke is now called the Princeton of the South.

- The black squirrels that roam around campus are a biology project gone wrong.

- Alexander Hall was originally designed as an architecture thesis. After the senior received an F on the thesis, he went on to become a wealthy architect and donated the building to Princeton on the condition that his thesis design would be used.

School Spirit

Princeton students and alumni can never be accused of not having school spirit. From making endless jokes about Harvard and Yale to coming back for annual reunions, Princeton is more than a four-year education, it is a lifetime legacy. An alumnus at a recent P-rade said, "The toughest thing about Princeton is not getting in. It is getting over it." While Princeton is not a school where all undergrads attend all of the football games, there is a constant aura of Princetonia. It is nearly impossible to pass through FitzRandolph Gates at graduation without owning at least one vibrant orange and black article of clothing. This spirit does not stop at the school level. Princeton undergrads also rally behind their residential colleges and continue to discuss who had the best experience. For example, Butler residents brag about their intramural prowess while Rocky residents make fun of Butler for its dorms and claim superiority because of their Gothic dorms.

Traditions

Baccalaureate Address

Baccalaureate is one of Princeton's most time-honored traditions. Originally referred to as a sermon, the Baccalaureate Address marks the end of Reunions and the start of Commencement activities for graduating seniors. Held in the University Chapel, recent speakers have included retiring Dean of Admission Fred Hargadon and e-Bay CEO Meg Whitman '77.

Beer Jackets

Traditionally made of white denim, beer jackets are part of the Reunions uniform for each class. This tradition began with a few members of the Class of 1912, who noticed that that the foam from their beers would spot their clothing. To avoid pricy cleaning charges, they developed the idea of a beer jacket, a jacket that could be worn to protect clothing from stains while drinking. The following year, the Class of 1913 adopted this tradition and wore their signature beer jackets throughout the spring. In recent times, the graduating class will vote on a design for their jacket, which is distributed during reading period of their final exam period.

Big Three Bonfire

The Bonfire is by no means a regular occurrence on Princeton's campus. According to tradition, a bonfire is to be built after Princeton's football team beats both Harvard and Yale, thus serving as a celebration of the much-coveted Big Three Title. Students construct the bonfire in the center of Cannon Green behind Nassau Hall.

Cane Spree

Organized to foster class spirit, Cane Spree is a series of athletic competitions pitting the entering freshman class and the sophomore class against each other. Traditionally, the event occurs at the end of the second week of classes. A tradition dating back to the 1860s, Cane Spree's competitions have changed, but the customary cane wrestling still remains. The victorious class gets the shirts from the other class.

Colors

Even after the Civil War, Princeton did not have official school colors. A member of the Class of 1869 suggested orange as a school color in honor of the Prince of Orange, William III of the House of Nassau, as Nassau Hall had been named for him. Orange was not adopted until Princeton students found success in a baseball game against of Yale students while wearing badges with orange ribbons.

Commencement Season

Commencement season at Princeton takes almost a week, starting with the annual alumni reunions, which begin the Thursday before commencement. The alumni parade, the P-rade, takes place Saturday morning, and the alumni leave campus the following day in time for the Baccalaureate Address to the graduating seniors and their families. Monday is dedicated to Class Day exercises, departmental receptions, and senior prom. Recent Class Day speakers include such Bill Cosby and Jerry Seinfeld. On Tuesday, commencement exercises include an invocation, the Latin salutatory, the conferring of degrees, the valedictory, a speech from the University's president, and the singing of "Old Nassau" before graduates pass through FitzRandolph Gate.

FitzRandolph Gate

Across Nassau Green is the all-important Nassau Street, the so-called "main drag" through town. In order to get into town from Nassau Hall, students must pass through the infamous FitzRandolph Gate. Legend has it that any student who passes out of the Gate before graduation will not graduate with his class or at all. Students take this very seriously, and it has become a rite of passage for graduating seniors to walk out the gates at the end of their graduation ceremony, which is held every year on Nassau Green.

Honor Code

Princeton's Honor System was adopted in 1893 at the demand of students. Some technical changes have been made to the system over the years, but the essential principles still remain. Students take responsibility for their academic integrity sign a pledge at the end of every paper and exam stating that they have neither given nor received assistance.

Locomotive

Princeton's oldest cheer, dating by some accounts from the 1890s, has the sound of a locomotive. It starts slowly and picks up speed and volume. This is a popular cheer during the annual P-rade.

Nude Olympics

Shortly after women began to enroll as Princeton undergraduates in the fall of 1969, the tradition of the Nude Olympics was born. During their sophomore year, the first completely coed class, the Class of 1973, participated in naked revelry in Holder Courtyard. Over the years, some aspects of the Nude Olympics have changed except for the central rules: the Nude Olympics would occur at midnight in Holder Courtyard during the first major snowfall of the year, and sophomores would participate. After much debate, the Nude Olympics was banned several years ago, and incoming students must sign a pledge agreeing not to participate.

Old Nassau

Princeton's alma mater is sung at the end of most campus events, including athletic events and Triangle shows. The song was composed by Harlan Page Peck, Class of 1862

P-rade

Formally, the Alumni Parade, the P-rade occurs the Saturday of class reunions. The twenty-fifth reunion class heads the parade, followed by each of alumni classes wearing their signature beer jackets. At the end of the P-rade, the graduating class runs onto Elm Drive to join the procession.

Reunions

Today, alumni reunions are the biggest alumni event of the year. As a time for lecture series, class gifts, and fanfare, campus becomes a sea of orange and black. Classes identify themselves by way of banners, blazers, and beer jackets. With thousands of alumni returning each year, alumni reunions have become one of Budweiser's biggest events of the year, with sleeping quarters for alumni all over campus.

Theft of the Nassau Hall Clapper

The bell in the tower of Nassau Hall used to ring at 9 p.m. to signal the freshman curfew. On the nights that the bell did not sound, freshmen would be allowed to stay out later. As early as the 1860s, freshmen would steal the clapper, and the bell would have to rung with a hammer. Throughout the years, it became almost an expectation for the freshman class to steal the bell's clapper, but the reward changed. Eventually, a victorious theft of the clapper would lead to the cancellation of early classes. The tradition ended when a member of the Class of 1995 fell from the bell tower while trying to steal the clapper his freshman year.

Finding a Job or Internship

The Lowdown On...
Finding a Job or Internship

Princeton's Office of Career Services offers plenty of resources to students who are looking for a job or internship, but students definitely have to take a pro-active approach during the process. Because Princeton students are so heavily recruited for banking and consulting positions, it often seems as if Career Services focuses all of their resources on students interested in those positions, but there are many services available to students who do not fall into those categories. Because of Princeton's strong alumni network, however, it is frequently networking that helps students get sought-after jobs and internships.

Advice

When you get to campus, make an appointment with an advisor at the Career Services Office to discuss your interests and develop a resume. Your advisor may be able to put you in touch with alumni who can advise you on good classes to take for your desired career and possibly invite you to trail them in their jobs for a day. Also, make sure to put yourself on the career email listserv so that you can get weekly updates about internships and jobs as well as upcoming programs, including career fairs and resume building workshops.

Career Center Resources & Services

- Career Assessment
- Career Counseling
- Career Workshops and Programs
- Job Search Assistance
- Internships
- Alumni Careers Network
- On-Campus Recruiting
- Graduate, Law, and Business School Advising
- Credentials Service
- Career Fairs
- Career Library
- CareerNews Listservs
- TigerTracks

AVERAGE SALARY INFORMATION

The Lowdown:
The following statistics represent average starting salaries for Princeton graduates by major.

Anthropology	$51,250
Art & Archaeology	$38,833
Astrophysical Sciences	$56,000
Chemical Engineering	$52,222
Chemistry	$47,333
Civil & Environmental Engineering	$48,600
Classics	$44,750
Comparative Literature	$44,667
Computer Science	$62,206
East Asian Studies	$45,000
Economics	$50,292
Ecology & Evolutionary Biology	$39,500
Electrical Engineering	$58,283
English	$38,100
History	$44,365
Mechanical & Aerospace Engineering	$52,578
Mathematics	$62,500
Molecular Biology	$49,571
Operations Research & Financial Engineering	$53,932
Philosophy	$47,125
Politics	$47,500
Psychology	$36,500
Religion	$55,750
Romance Languages	$58,500
Sociology	$52,250
Woodrow Wilson School	$48,005

Alumni

The Lowdown On...
Alumni

Website:
http://alumni.princeton.edu

Office:
Alumni Council of Princeton
University
Maclean House
P.O. Box 291
Princeton, NJ 08544-0291
alco@Princeton.EDU
(609) 258-1900

Services Available
Online Alumni Directory
Email Services
Transcript Requests
Alumni Schools Committee
Resources

→

The Alumni Schools Committee (ASC), which includes over 5,000 volunteers, interviews applicants in an effort to help the Admissions Office select the members of the incoming class. Over 10,000 interviews are conducted each year.

Alumni Careers Network

The Alumni Careers Network (ACN) is a database of Princeton alumni who have volunteered to provide other alumni as well as students with professional advice, site visits, and job and project assistance. For students and professionals, this is an invaluable resource, as it puts Princetonians from several generations in touch to provide career advice and assistance.

@princeton Courseware

Princeton alumni have the opportunity to continue their education online by way of the @princeton courseware. Each semester, distinguished professors conduct an online course, complete with video lectures in some instances. This is one of the many ways that Princeton promotes lifelong learning.

Alumni Colleges

Several times a year, Princeton sponsors trips to locations around the world for alumni. Led by noted professors and staff members, recent trips have included Alaska, the Amazon, and Ireland. These trips draw from the experience of the leaders and serve not only as a vacation for alumni but also as education.

Major Alumni Events:

Princeton's biggest alumni events include Alumni Day, Reunions, and Homecoming. Homecoming takes place in the fall and includes class gatherings and tailgates before some Tiger football. Alumni Day is considered a mid-winter alumni celebration during which alumni return to campus for lectures by distinguished faculty. The Woodrow Wilson Award and James Madison Medal are given , and the day ends with a Service of Remembrance. Reunions, lasting several days, are Princeton's biggest alumni event. From fireworks to lectures to the P-rade, Princetonians take reunions very seriously, and attendance is always impressive.

Alumni Publications:

Princeton Alumni Weekly

Princeton Alumni Weekly, or PAW, is sent to all Princeton alumni for no charge. It includes regular columns about campus life, engaging letters to the editor, feature articles, and alumni updates.

Did You Know?

Famous Princeton Alums—

James Baker (Class of '52), former Secretary of State

Jeff Bezos (Class of '86), founder of Amazon.com

Bill Bradley (Class of '65), basketball star and politician

Dean Cain (Class of '88), actor in "Lois and Clark"

David Duchovny (Class of '82), actor in "The X Files"

John Foster Dulles (Class of '35), former Secretary of State

Steve Forbes (Class of '70), Forbes Magazine President and Editor-in-Chief

Bill Frist (Class of '74), Senate Majority Leader

Lisa Najeeb Halaby (Class of '76), Queen Noor of Jordan

James Madison (Class of 1771), former President of the United States

Ralph Nader (Class of '55), consumer advocate

Donald Rumsfeld (Class of '54), Secretary of Defense

Brooke Shields (Class of '87), actress in *The Blue Lagoon*

George Shultz (Class of '42), former Secretary of State

James Stewart (Class of '32), actor in *It's a Wonderful Life*

Meg Whitman (Class of '77), CEO of eBay

Student Organizations

STUDENT ORGANIZATIONS –

(This is only a brief sampling of the clubs and organizations offered; a full listing is available at *www.princeton.edu/odus/ student_organizations/org_list_public.html*)

A Fuego - Club to promote the study and practice of Latin Dance.

American Foreign Policy - www.princeton.edu/~afp – Publication that covers a host of

Black Arts Company - www.princeton.edu/~bac - Platform for students to express the

College Democrats - www.princeton.edu/~pudems

College Replublicans – www.princeton.edu/~pucolrep

Expressions Dance Company - www.princeton.edu/~lesexp – Dance group that performs two dance shows yearly of jazz, modern, ballet, hip hop, lyrical and tap pieces

Gallery, Princeton - www.princeton.edu/~gallery - Publication of Princeton students and affiliated art work

Ideas in Action - www.princeton.edu/~ideas - Promote socio-political awareness through lectures, forums, debates

Infinity, Ltd. - www.princeton.edu/~infinity - Princeton's science fiction and fantasy club

Juggling Club – www.princeton.edu/~juggling

Katzenjammers - www.princeton.edu/~pukatz - The Ivy League's oldest co-ed a cappella group

Manna Christian Fellowship - www.princeton.edu/~manna - Non-denominational organization

Muslim Students Association

Naacho - Indian dancing

Native Americans at Princeton - www.princeton.edu/~naap

Pride Alliance - www.princeton.edu/~pride - For gay, lesbian, bisexual, transgender, queer, questioning and straight-ally students.

Princeton Tory - www.princeton.edu/~tory - Monthly magazine covering campus and world issues from a moderate to conservative viewpoint

Princeton Triangle Club - www.princeton.edu/~triangle - Student-run musical comedy theater troupe

Stripes - www.princeton.edu/~stripes - Sketch comedy group that writes and performs comedic skits

Theatre Intime - www.princeton.edu/~intime - Student run independent theater with dedicated theatrical facilities

University Film Organization - www.princeton.edu/~ufo - Society of students dedicated to showing both popular, artistic, and international films

Whig-Cliosophic Society - www.princeton.edu/~whigclio - The Nation's oldest college political, literary, and debating society

Yavneh House - www.princeton.edu/~yavneh - Organization that facilitates social & religious activities for observant Jews on campus

The Best & The Worst

The Ten BEST Things About Princeton:

1	Strong academic program
2	Focus on campus undergraduate life
3	Renovated dorms
4	Tradition and strong alumni programs
5	Sunday brunch at Forbes
6	Eating clubs for upperclass dining
7	Senior nights at the Annex
8	Safe campus
9	Houseparties
10	Sitting out on Alexander Beach on a sunny day

The Ten **Worst** Things About Princeton:

1 The relative isolation of the town

2 Rainy springs

3 Old, outdated dorms

4 Crowded Stephens Fitness Center

5 Rare Big Three Bonfires

6 Academic advising system for underclassmen

7 High price of stores and restaurants in town

8 Boring precepts

9 Pizza night in the dining halls

10 Non-English speaking TAs and preceptors

Visiting Princeton

The Lowdown On...
Visiting Princeton

Hotel Information

In Princeton:

Nassau Inn

www.nassauinn.com

Palmer Square

Princeton, NJ

(609) 921-7500, (800) 862-7728

Distance from Campus:
Walking distance

Price Range: $190-$230

Peacock Inn

peacockinn.com

20 Bayard Lane

Princeton, NJ

(609) 924-1707

Distance from Campus:
Walking distance

Price Range: $125

Route 1, North of Campus: Courtyard by Marriot

www.marriott.com

U.S. Route 1 and Mapleton Rd.

(609) 716-9100,
(800) 321-2211

Distance from Campus:
2 miles

Price Range: $170

Days Inn

www.daysinn.com

U.S. Route 1 and Raymond Road

Monmouth Junction, NJ

(732) 329-4555,
(800) 325-2525.

Distance from Campus:
4 miles

Price Range: $60

Doral Forrestal Hotel and Spa

www.doralforrestal.com

Princeton Forrestal Center

Princeton, NJ

(609) 452-7800,
(800) 222-1131.

Distance from Campus:
5 miles

Price Range: $154-$240

Extended StayAmerica

www.extstay.com

3450 Brunswick Pike

Princeton, NJ

(609) 919-9000

Distance from Campus:
5 miles

Price Range: $79(weekday),
$69(weekend)

Holiday Inn

www.holiday-inn.com

100 Independence Way

Princeton, NJ

(609) 520-1200.

Distance from Campus:
5 miles

Price Range: $90

Radisson Hotel Princeton

www.radisson.com

4355 U.S. Route 1 at Ridge Road

Princeton, NJ

(609) 452-2400,
(800) 333-3333.

Distance from Campus:
5 miles

Price Range: $130

Summerfield Suites Hotel

www.wyndham.com

4375 U.S. Route 1

Princeton, NJ

(609) 951-0009,
(800) 833-4353.

Distance from Campus:
5 miles

Price Range: $100

Westin Princeton at Forrestal

www.starwood.com/westin

201 Village Boulevard

Princeton, NJ

(609) 520-6211, fax
(609) 452-0927

Distance from Campus:
5 miles

Price Range: $120-$245

Route 1, South of Campus:

AmeriSuites

www.amerisuites.com/

3565 U.S. Route 1

Princeton , NJ

(609) 720-0200,
(800) 833-1516

Distance from Campus:
3 miles

Price Range: $130-$150

Howard Johnson's Motor Lodge

www.hojo.com

U.S. Route 1

Lawrenceville, NJ

(609) 896-1100,
(800) IGO-HOJO

Distance from Campus:
8 miles

Price Range: $115

Hyatt Regency

www.hyatt.com

102 Carnegie Center, U.S. Route 1

Princeton, NJ

(609) 987-1234,
(800) 233-1234

Distance from Campus:
2 miles

Price Range: $160-$190

McIntosh Motor Inn

3270 U.S. Route 1

Lawrenceville, NJ

(609) 896-3700,
(800) 444-2775

Distance from Campus:
6 miles

Price Range: Sunday-
Thursday $74.95; Friday-
Saturday $84.95

Q "Princeton is what you make of it. I threw myself into extra activities to meet a lot of new people freshman year. Some of my hallmates threw themselves into their work and quickly found themselves **isolated and without a true support network.** They grades may have been better freshmen year, but I wonder if they were ever really happy at Princeton, because they could have spent four years in a library anywhere."

Q "It has been, by far, **the best time of my life,** both socially and intellectually. I really wish I could stay here forever."

Q "Looking back on it, **the decision to attend Princeton is one of the best I ever made.** I have no doubt that I have received the best undergraduate education available in this country. I have had the opportunity to work with some excellent professors, write a 100-page thesis, dance with friends until the sun comes up, sample four types of veggie burgers, and discuss civil liberties at three in the morning over espresso with a friend who is wrangling horses this fall and one who was the head of the campus Christian outreach. While I might have wished at points that I were somewhere else because of the stresses of the academic program, the rigor of the academic experience at Princeton has helped shape me as an individual, taught me to have personal expectations, and led me into adulthood."